The Churkendôôse Anthology

The Churkendôôse Anthology

True Stories of Triumph over Neurological Dysfunction

Insights into the
Holistic **A**pproach to **N**euro**D**evelopment
and **L**earning **E**fficiency
(HANDLE®)

Commentary by Judith Bluestone
Edited by Lisa Brenner

The
Churkendôôse
Anthology

True Stories of Triumph
over Neurological Dysfunction

Insights into the
Holistic Approach to NeuroDevelopment and Learning Efficiency
(HANDLE®)

ISBN 0-9720235-5-0
Library of Congress Control Number: 2002105241

Reprinted with permission by
Sapphire Enterprises, LLC
1300 Dexter Avenue North, Suite 110
The Casey Family Building
Seattle, Washington 98109
(206) 204-6000

Orignally Published by: The HANDLE Institute

The names in some stories have been changed to protect the
identities of the persons involved.

Cover design by Kristin M. Adams

Grateful acknowledgement is made to the following for permission to
reprint previously published material: *Welcome to Holland*
Copyright ©1987 by Emily Perl Kingsley. All rights reserved.
Reprinted with permission of the author.

Printed in the United States of America

CONTENTS

Part 4: I have more brains than I have luck

Part 5: What ARE you, anyway?

Part 6: I can't walk, I wouldn't take the chance, but if you give me some music, I'll go into my dance

Part 7: Making friends can be a pleasure

Epilogue: Without "always," "never" and "impossible"

Appendix A: Selected exercises

Appendix B: Clinical procedures

FOREWORD

As I reflect on Judith Bluestone and the HANDLE approach, I am reminded of Dr. Oliver Sacks and "Awakenings." The parallels are exquisite: the in-depth observation, the focus on behavior rather than diagnosis, the creative approaches to understanding and intervention.

My mind turns next to my long association with Judith as the younger daughter of close friends, Reva and Henry Bluestone; Judith's own struggles with bringing forth her uncanny creativity and brilliance; Judith, our first teacher at Glenwood School for adolescents with different learning challenges; Judith's discoveries during her work in and around Kiryat Shmona in the North of Israel; and finally, her remarkable work in developing the HANDLE® approach and founding The HANDLE Institute.

One essential element in HANDLE's program is to set aside judgment about what is a "right" diagnosis, and instead, implement intense observation in a probing search for the roots of dysfunctional behavior. The unfortunate emphasis of many is the label; is this ADD, ADHD, Asperger's Syndrome, autism? Meanwhile, the person is lost. HANDLE sees each as an individual, insists on respect for the client and seeks to free the potential, the creative energy, that has been blocked.

The search for the key to unlock individual expression is that essential beginning of discovery, the unearthing which leads to a program, customized and therapeutic. The range of application seems to know no bounds and may be viewed as questionable by many in the field.

Yet, after reviewing the case histories of those who have

been ostracized, rejected, deeply hurt, confused and confusing, the reaching of new life is revealed. To read about Leah who said, after her HANDLE work, "I'm just waking up." Or to learn of Gulliver—a boy helped to bring out his cry, who said, "When I do cry a lot I do start to feel sorry"—awakening to recognize the feeling, and say the words. The HANDLE approach utilizes "user friendly" methods to open opportunities for self-expression and levels of recognition and respect previously unknown.

I am indeed impressed by Judith's discovery of those "missing pieces of the puzzle." Beyond that, Judith is able to teach her method to clients, their parents and guardians, and to other practitioners. The applications of the HANDLE approach must be recognized.

It is with deep appreciation and pride that I endorse the work and achievements of Judith Bluestone, her colleagues and especially the fortunate ones who have, through HANDLE, found their way.

—Melvin E. Allerhand, Ph.D.

Dr. Allerhand holds an ABPP in Clinical, Child Psychology and is the author of Adaptation and Adaptability—a follow up study of 50 Bellefaire Boys. He has conducted research in cognitive development, including an early study of the HeadStart program. He is an Associate Professor of Clinical-Child Psychology at Case Western Reserve University, consultant to public and private schools and learning centers, founder and consultant to Glenwood School for children with learning problems and co-founder of Tree of Knowledge Learning Center.

In Gratitude

I n *The Churkendoose Anthology*, I must give thanks to a vast number of people who have made this volume possible, and who have made the promulgation of HANDLE possible, and who have made possible my being here, able to give HANDLE to others.

The many pediatricians, neurologists, obstetricians, orthopedic surgeons, orthodontists, prosthodontists, maxillofacial surgeons, internists and ear-nose-and-throat specialists, without whose intervention I would probably not be alive, able to walk and speak and chew and swallow and hear.

Yael Shany, a homeopath and reflexologist par excellence, who virtually saved my life in 1987 in Israel and helped guide me through another serious medical challenge in 1992 in Seattle.

A few undaunted teachers who allowed me to do what I needed to do as I was coping with my most serious neurodevelopmental issues in the early grades, especially Mrs. Quilliams (whose first name I have forgotten) who endured my most bizarre behaviors with a smile and recognized my brilliance. And three mature classmates who sacrificed their free time during many recesses at Oxford Elementary School in order to ensure my safety and well-being—Diana Veith, Joann Shepherd, and Carol Lynn Morris.

Didi Lombardi, my next-door neighbor, who had Cerebral Palsy, and was my only playmate until her family moved away. Didi and I stretched the boundaries of our disabilities, taught one another to jump rope, and rolled on the grass in laughter and tears over all of our stumbles along the way.

An eighth grade social studies teacher, Edwin Paller, who was also staff advisor of the Wiley Junior High School newspaper, who heard my soul speak to him, who believed in me, and entrusted me with an editorial position that none of my peers thought I should receive.

Hessie Schrieber and Nikki Branson and Rena Bonder and Michael Klein, who provided me the four most enduring close friendships that I have ever had, and with whom I regret having lost contact many years ago.

Garry Handelman, who provided me occasions of respite and shared recluse whenever the physical and emotional pains of my tormented teen years were more than I could bear alone.

Mel and Revel Allerhand who, for nearly 50 years, have provided me the comfort of knowing I could, in their presence, be and say and do anything that my soul needed in order to gain fulfillment and respite. They had the difficult position of bearing the confidences of my mother, who was Revel's best friend, and my confidences as well, especially since so often it was my troubled existence that bore so heavily on my mother's heart.

Dr. James J. McCarthy, my advisor and mentor as I worked on my master's program in the department of Counseling and Behavioral Studies at the University of Wisconsin in Madison—who agreed to stretch beyond his own area of comfort to allow me to explore more fully the effect of neurological impairments on learning.

Dr. E. Christine Kris, the core professor who supported my doctoral work in applied neuroscience with great excitement for the new ground I was breaking, although it challenged some of her own long-held tenets.

Leah Amit, Mooli Lahad and Hevatzelet Shimshovich, who in their respective communities in Israel entrusted me with the development of programs for early childhood special education, during which time I created the basis of the assessment tools and therapeutic activities that have evolved into HANDLE.

The many educators, occupational therapists, physical therapists, psychological counselors, developmental optometrists, naturopaths, and others who have worked collaboratively with me, allowing me to expand my understanding of human dysfunction and to discern the elements that are necessary for efficient therapeutic procedures.

The much greater number of professionals who have questioned me about the approach and forced me to be able to articulate my theories and practices in a way that could meet their criticism.

Susie Hepner and Elinor Kriegsmann, Trina Westerlund and Judy Belk, the first four professionals in the Pacific Northwest to listen and believe that perhaps my yet un- named approach could actually augment their respective services for brain injured adults, children with disorders of language and learning, and children with severe disorders of behavior and learning.

The Directors who are currently serving on the board of directors of The HANDLE Institute, and those whose vision brought them to support my work from the inception of The HANDLE Institute. In particular, Wesley Lachman, whose generous offer of volunteer help to form The HANDLE Insti- tute, was the impetus to the creation of this nonprofit entity to promulgate the HANDLE approach. And Jim Nibblett whose support has been a felt presence throughout the be- ginning years of the Institute, and who continues to offer help in any way he can to ensure that HANDLE endures. Joe Parr, whose commitment to our mission and generosity in giving of himself and enlisting help of his friends has, time after time, allowed the Institute to remain viable. And most directly, in relation to this volume, Lisa Brenner, without whose assistance I could not have collected and compiled the stories, nor brought this work to publication.

Kristin Adams, who deserves special thanks for the graphic arts that make this volume the aesthetic piece that it is. And to our proofreaders, Claire Rothenberg and Vivian Zoller.

The staff of The HANDLE Institute and the volunteers who have borne the growing pains and the uncertainty of our financial existence, with the conviction that the work must continue, and they persist. Even to those whose per- sistence did not last, I am grateful for the help they did pro- vide when they had the strength.

Those who have come to study with me, especially those who have "gone the distance" to become Certified HANDLE Practitioners, and by doing so say that they believe fully in the approach and in its ability to endure and to help others. Particularly to Cathy Stingley, who moved into uncharted territory when she began to assist me in training others.

The innumerable individuals and families who have trusted me with their most precious treasures and their most horrific fears—the lives of my clients, crying out for help. I am sure that I have learned more from all of you than you will ever know.

My family:

My son, Matthew Saunders, who became my caretaker when he was not quite five years old, after I was seriously injured in an automobile accident, and who took care of himself and me repeatedly as my health continued to fail in one weird way after another until I got a handle on my own immune system and other various disorders. Matthew, himself, is currently completing his doctorate in Population Genetics. Possibly, collaborative research between geneticists and clinicians working with neurodevelopmental disorders may someday prove that the very genes that cause specific neurological disorders, if not altered artificially, may also provide the basis for specific gifts, such as those given to me.

My older sister, Marlene Suliteanu, an occupational therapist, who translated for me when I was two and three and four years old and beyond, at times when others could not understand my mumbled jargon. It is Marlene who, for over 30 years, urged me to publish and teach others the approach I had developed, and who only a couple of years ago decided to take up the gauntlet herself and become a Certified HANDLE® Practitioner. She continues to provide me with a leaning post when the vastness of the work, and especially the social commitments of what I have developed overwhelm me.

My parents, who spent tens of thousands of hours and pre-inflation dollars to seek out specialists and provide me treatments that they felt had a chance of helping me overcome my many neurodevelopmental problems.

More than that, my mother, Reva Bluestone, who died nearly 13 years ago, showed me and others that it is possible to achieve what you really want, despite adversity. And she, together with my father, Henry Bluestone, demonstrated by example that all people are worthy of respect, and that as long as an individual had enough to meet his or her own most basic needs it was incumbent to give what he or she could to others according to their need.

My father gave me several other gifts during my childhood—gifts that have kept me in good stead throughout my life:

♦ A sense of humor and ability to laugh at myself and not at others.

♦ The desire to achieve academic excellence in every

field that I study.

♦ The trust that I will listen to divergent thought and then form the right decision for myself.

♦ The absence from my vocabulary of three words and of three concepts: Always. Never. Impossible. From Dad's scientific viewpoint, there is nothing you can say will always be as it is at this point in time. Similarly, there is nothing that you can proclaim, definitely, will never happen. And to claim that something is "impossible" only means that no one has yet documented doing it. With those three words and concepts stricken, I knew that my future was only as limited as my ability to persevere. And perseverance is a gift that I have been given in rare abundance.

More directly and more recently, it was my father's generous donation to The HANDLE Institute that enabled me to take enough time away from income producing work to finish this book and to begin writing a more theoretical book on the principles and practices of HANDLE.

But it is this book, *The Churkendoose Anthology*, that I felt needed to be the first book on HANDLE, since it is the Churkendeese of the world who have provided me the inspiration.

So it is to all of the families whose stories fill these pages that I offer my deepest gratitude, and say *thank you* for bringing this work to fruition.

—*Judith Bluestone*

INTRODUCTION

"What are you, anyway?" This question torments the newborn Churkendoose as the other barnyard creatures in *The Story of the Churkendoose* fearfully and hastily contemplate if and how to allow this unusual creature born in their midst to be a welcome member of their community.[1] This question tormented me as I was growing up, as my parents took me from doctor to doctor, from therapist to therapist, trying to find out why I was so small, so sickly, so delayed in my speech, so uncoordinated, so standoffish, so temperamental, so compulsive, so defiant, so peculiar in aspects of my appearance, and so brilliant—all the while looking for ways to help me gain the health and the basic skills necessary to be a truly functional member of society. So when the Churkendoose announces, "This is MY story. I'm the Churkendoose. Part chicken, turkey, duck and goose," he is speaking for me and for so many other children and adults around the world.

The Story of the Churkendoose depicts the birth of an animal like no other. The other animals can't identify with him. They are threatened by his ability to recite poetry and tap dance, and frightened by his outward appearance: having only one ear, wobbly legs, and looking unlike anything

---

[1]*The Churkendoose Part Chicken, Turkey, Duck and Goose* is a children's book written by Ben Ross Berenberg and published by Wonder Books in 1946. A few years later, Decca records, with lyricist Alec Wilder, produced a musical rendition of this story. The recording, titled *The Story of the Churkendoose*, featured Ray Bolger as the primary recording artist. The story helps children realize the wonders of diversity by using the parable of the barnyard to stand for any community. Both the book and the recording are out-of-print, but The HANDLE Institute obtained limited copyrights for the recording in order to bring this important story back to the English-speaking children of the world.

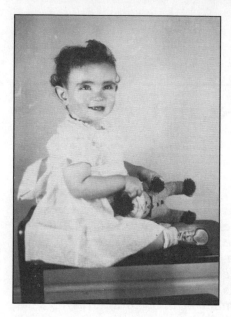

At 12 months. It's easy to observe my lopsided mouth, an early indicator of some of my cranial nerve and maxillo-facial problems.

Some people might miss the locked knees and tight squeezing, both reflective of a problem that is developing in my middle and inner ears, affecting their ability to read the subtle messages from my body about its position in space (proprioception.)

For many years after these early photos,
as some of my problems became more obvious, I avoided
being in front of a camera whenever possible.

they had ever seen. Before throwing the newborn out with absolutely no nurturing, the animals meet to discuss his fate. They do not allow the Churkendoose to participate in this meeting, as they feel it is none of his concern. They will dictate their decision to him. Those of us who have been poked and prodded, questioned and tested, and then told to wait outside while the experts tell our parents or caregivers what they have decided should be done to us or for us—we know, like the Churkendoose, how disempowering this process is.

While waiting to learn the decision that was reached, the Churkendoose wanders over to a puddle, and looks at his unusual shape, even more distorted by the reflections in the water. In tears, he ponders, "Can it be that I am such a sight, that when others see me they take fright?" He goes on to ask, "Are the hippopotami any handsomer than I?" which is answered in the refrain of, "It depends on how you look at things." Then, getting beyond the issue of his unusual outward appearance, the Churkendoose ruminates on the fact that difference is a natural phenomenon, "Does the green grass ask the sky so blue 'I'm green. Why aren't you green, too?'" And that there is a purpose for every thing in this universe, "'My skin makes leather,' snorts the bull. The sheep replies 'I grow wool.'" But it is not enough that he sings out, "Each one has its special use. And I'm sure there's one for the Churkendoose." He soulfully laments, "There *must* be one for the Churkendoose." And just then, he hears shrieks of terror from the henhouse.

His purpose reveals itself. In the story, his first purpose is to frighten away the fox that is trying to catch and devour the barnyard creatures, and then, to teach the other animals some of the things he knows. But, of course, his real purpose is to teach the others to be nonjudgmental and to respect individual differences, since only then can each member of society grow and become truly fulfilled.

So, as we were planning to compile and publish the stories of a few of the unique and gifted children and adults who have been helped by HANDLE over the years, my working title for the book was *The Churkendoose Anthology*. I have always felt myself to be a Churkendoose, and affectionately view as Churkendeese most of those people with neurodevelopmental differences with whom I have come in contact. What better title for a book that reflects, through true stories, triumph over difficult neurological conditions?

It remains *The Churkendoose Anthology,* and in my vision this is Volume 1, to be followed, I am sure, by an outpouring of stories for future volumes, as HANDLE spreads its theories and practices of nonjudgmental assessment and Gentle Enhancement® therapy to those in need around the world.

If my parents had not found the Decca LP album of *The Story of the Churkendoose* and the Golden Book with the same story, I am not sure I would have had the strength of conviction to be Just Me—the person who I was and who I am—against the pressure of those who were embarrassed by me, afraid of me, exasperated by me, and in some ways in awe of me. My own family is included in that group of people. My mother and older sister were embarrassed by my lack of social graces, by my lack of physical coordination. They were, at times, fearful of what my under-socialized impulsive mouth might say, with little regard for the feelings of others. My father frequently joined my mother and sister in their exasperation with me, especially when I would not allow them to finish sentences before I responded and when I could not control compulsive behaviors that annoyed everyone around me. And yet they were each in awe of some of my abilities—my eidetic memory for things I saw, my rote memory of songs and scripts, my precocious ability to read and write, the soulful poetry I wrote when I was nine and ten years old, my powers of concentration, my ability to find whatever had been lost, my genius with puzzles and games of logic.

This intermingling of challenges and talents, of deformities and resolution, of stubbornness and flexibility, of creative synthesis and analytical deduction—this wild mix of qualities that have formed my life has helped me create the HANDLE approach. And the families whose lives HANDLE has changed over the years have given me the strength to continue with this work, without recognition and frequently without pay, but with the immeasurable rewards you can't help but feel as you read these stories.

I developed HANDLE during 25 years of professional work as a learning disabilities specialist who branched out to apply neuroscience to virtually all forms of learning—social, academic, language, motor, inward responses, and more. And in the 10 years since I began to teach others the basic approach of HANDLE, the approach has continued to grow, to incorporate changes in the human experience, from computers to new therapy techniques, from changing forms of environmental influences to evolving nutritional considerations, ever seeking the explanations for the seemingly magical events that occur when people embark on and journey through a HANDLE program.

The greatest rewards that I have received have been in the last several years, as others whom I have trained to be HANDLE practitioners have performed the "magic" of HANDLE. I have been able to capture and articulate and teach those things that many thought were intuitive gifts, unique to me. And so now, we are seeing a slowly growing band of Certified HANDLE Practitioners reaching out to their local communities to help the Churkendeese who turn to them. In this volume you will meet 30 Churkendeese, some of whom I have never met other than through their stories. As I first read their stories, I was in awe that I had been given a gift that had reached so far and had helped so profoundly.

The dispersing of my gift is happening just in time. The fox *is* in the henhouse, chasing everyone, with labels of disorders that he knows not how to alleviate, with medications that mask symptoms without understanding what the symptomatic behaviors are telling us, and with measures to control behaviors without realizing that most of those behaviors are intuitive attempts at either self-healing or self-protection from an environment that is hostile or harmful to those with profound neurodevelopmental differences.

So many treatment modalities are emerging at this time. And the public is lately coming to realize that while there is certainly an important place for western medicine and technological advances, these cannot replace more traditional approaches that honor the natural processes of development and healing. We are moving into a period of integrated medicine, and with that shift, the bases of HANDLE as applied neuroscience are becoming more widely accepted. HANDLE can complement almost any approach that is respectful of the human being and human responses. It cannot work in conjunction with those approaches that are disrespectful of body or mind; approaches that demand the body sacrifice time and energy to the point of physical and emotional exhaustion, approaches that seek arbitrarily to mask symptoms, approaches that desire to control disturbing behaviors to make others more comfortable without taking into account what the symptoms are there to tell us.

With so many different approaches to healing, HANDLE, not unlike the Churkendoose, makes a unique contribution to the world community. Each of the families in these stories represents dozens of other families who have not yet stepped forward to share their tragedies and their triumphs. And all these families feel that, although they have tried other approaches to cure or resolve the difficulties they have faced, it was HANDLE that had the greatest impact on their movement from dysfunction to function.

THE HANDLE APPROACH

So, what is this approach that has given innumerable families facing diverse challenges and living in vastly discrepant cultures a handle on their lives? The name HANDLE is an acronym for:

Holistic **A**pproach to **N**euro**D**evelopment and **L**earning **E**fficiency.

"**H**olistic" refers to viewing the numerous interdependent body-mind influences within each individual as his or her systems respond to the multi-faceted elements in the entire environment. "Holistic" acknowledges the possible causal roles of chemicals (including pharmaceutical versions), allergens, nutritional deficits (especially the lack of water and essential fatty acids) and toxins of any kind. It encompasses use of color and lighting and sound in the environment and considers lifestyle factors, such as TV and video games, that have replaced active movement and decreased the demand on our imaginations (creativity) as graphic media provides us a virtual reality. "Holistic" acknowledges our tendency to stay at home and indoors while we engage in online shopping and telecommutes.

"**A**pproach" means that HANDLE is a paradigm—a set of guiding principles rather than a set of exercises or techniques—that is unified by applied neuroscience deduced from developmental behavior, including the evidence that the body organizes the brain, not vice versa. The approach incorporates practices from many related disciplines. Certified HANDLE Practitioners identify, and then gently enhance, weak areas of neurological function, and immediately honor signs of stress in the client's body, and as such, customize programs for each client individually.

"NeuroDevelopment" refers not to a given sequence of accrued skills but to an *interactive hierarchy* of nervous systems' functions, with emphasis on the role of the cranial nerves and autonomic nervous system rather than isolated functions in particular sites in the brain. Development is a lifelong process that relies on neuroplasticity, the ability of the brain and the rest of the nervous system(s) to reshape themselves according to the stimulation they receive, and including, again, the effects of nutrition, toxins, etc.

"Learning" is the process of using sensory, motor, social and emotional input to realign output into behavior, sometimes successfully and sometimes less so. Both learning and brain structure continue to develop from shortly after conception until the moment of death. Learning, as development, is cyclical. When we see spirals in normal development, we acknowledge this. When we experience spirals in the learning processes of people with special needs we forget that regression is a normal part of development. It simply means that the seemingly lost behavior was not well enough internalized to appear automatically, and for now, the body-brain has another priority.

"Efficiency" goes far beyond effective performance, as it refers to the brain expending the least amount of energy and experiencing minimum stress as it works to orchestrate how we accomplish tasks. For example, sitting still in class may require so much effort to ignore hypersensitive sensations as legs press against the chair, that no energy is left over to attend to the lessons. The student can sit still, but at what cost? Effective in sitting still? Sure. And socially acceptable too. But efficient in learning? No chance.

As HANDLE discerns functions through the observational assessment of a wide range of activities, it also defines outcomes in life, not in tasks. Then therapy addresses the root causes of maladaptive or unsuccessful behaviors. With Gentle Enhancement to encourage neurodevelopmental integration, the body, not the therapist, directs the individual to perform tasks optimally; efficiently, not just effectively.

When people encounter HANDLE theories and practices in depth, the most frequently voiced comment is, "That makes so much sense!" And then they ask me, "Why haven't we heard of this approach before?"

To promulgate the work of HANDLE, I founded The HANDLE Institute in 1994, and in October of that year, it was incorporated as a nonprofit organization. Yet, despite the quiet clamor for sharing the work more broadly, until the publication of this book, the Institute has refrained from publicizing the benefits of HANDLE for a number of reasons. Many people, concerned about the scientific basis of a methodology, demand research and do not accept the thousands of case files with anecdotal evidence. Currently the University of Washington and Harborview Medical Center in Seattle are engaged in just such an independent study, but we do not know when the results will be made public. And so, we have finally decided that the stories cannot wait to be told until the independent research on this new diagnostic and treatment modality is published.

In addition, we refrained because we were concerned that many people, reduced to hopelessness, might flock to seek HANDLE to help them move out from this despair. We wanted to find a way to share the gifts of HANDLE that would not feed on these desperate situations. We needed to wait until we had the prospects of telling families that it is possible that there will be a Certified HANDLE Practitioner able to service their needs in the near future, that programs have been piloted to bring HANDLE into preschools and public schools and clinics that engage in neurorehabilitation, that some members of the medical profession have embraced HANDLE and are engaged in independent research to demonstrate its effects on the brain, and other members of the medical community have sought advanced HANDLE training so they can employ its observational assessment to better understand the problems they are faced with daily. This is becoming a reality, as professionals across the country and around the world are moving through HANDLE training, and rehabilitation centers and schools are seeking in-service training for their staff and are seeking funds for pilot projects to incorporate HANDLE in their work.

THE CHURKENDOOSE ANTHOLOGY IS BORN

As I have been hatching this project, with the unwavering and energetic editorial assistance of Lisa Brenner, there have been many questions to answer. Families who made contributions wanted to know how long the stories should be, and whether they should write them in the first or second or third person. True to the basic philosophy of HANDLE, we told them unequivocally that these were *their* stories, to be written as their expression brought forth. The only thing we did tell families was that there was a cut-off date for inclusion in this volume. Some families did not meet that deadline. It does not make their stories any less significant, and we hope to publish them in a subsequent volume.

I began the anthology with stories of adults, since so frequently it is the adults in our society whose problems seem hopeless, who are written off, while we tend to provide children a little more opportunity to develop. We have more hope for our children, because we understand that as they grow, their bodies and brains change. What people do not accept as readily is that this process of the brain's adaptation to the stimulation it receives is a life-long process with the name neuroplasticity. Our nervous systems are designed to mold themselves to our experiences. And so, in this volume, I decided to first demonstrate this process in stories of adults, then the changes that occur in the children whose stories you will read will be more credible.

The progress of some of our clients may seem miraculous. In the sense that it is a marvelous phenomenon to observe and more so to take part in, yes, these stories represent miracles. But more importantly, they demonstrate how one approach can help resolve a wide array of seemingly disparate disorders in people of all ages. And it can do this naturally, without the use of medication or expensive highly technological equipment. In fact, one of our interns was drawn to HANDLE particularly for that reason, as she intends to bring HANDLE to the underdeveloped countries in Africa where the earth below one's feet and the sky overhead may be the only materials given to work with—those and the human beings who inhabit those lands and their amazing spirits that reside within.

The purpose of this book is to encourage a paradigm shift, one that moves people from looking at specific behaviors as symptoms of a specific labeled disorder. We cannot treat labels. If there were any one medication or behavior modification approach to treat autism or dyslexia or attentional disorders or mood disorders, we would no longer have these problems in our midst. But instead, the problems are increasing, seemingly in exponential fashion.

With *The Churkendoose Anthology*, we hope to make a notable contribution by helping people realize that the behaviors *are* symptoms, not of a labeled disorder, but of weaknesses or irregularities in parts of the nervous systems—central nervous system, autonomic nervous system, enteric nervous system, and energetic fields that form the basis of all of the information we receive from the external world and process internally. It is only by discerning the strengths and weaknesses in each person's systems and then employing their strengths to gently enhance their weaknesses—only in that way can we truly create function from dysfunction, order from chaos. Enough said at this point. The stories will speak for themselves...

PART 1

TEACHING THE
DUCK HOW TO
TAP DANCE

—Ben Ross Berenberg
The Churkendoose
Part Chicken, Turkey, Duck and Goose

READY FOR A CHANGE
CATHY STINGLEY, CERTIFIED HANDLE PRACTITIONER

The phone call came at just the right time. I had reached a point, after eleven years with the mental health clinic, that I was ready for a change. I had been thinking about it and, though I had many ideas, I had not come to a conclusion about what I should do next.

Next... every six to ten years I found myself ready to move on, to find something new and different to do. There had been the preschool, firefighting, advanced Emergency Medical Technician work, training Emergency Medical Technicians and then mental health. Did I want to go back to one of these? Did I want to do something with my music? Was I ready for something entirely new?

So, when Jessica Anderson's mother called to ask if I would go to Vashon Island in Puget Sound, Washington, it sounded like the perfect opportunity; five and a half weeks on an island accessible only by ferry or by plane. I could take care of Jessica, meditate on career opportunities and leave myself open to anything that came along.

Jessica and I knew each other from a few years back when I had been her Activity Therapist in Homer, Alaska. She was now fourteen. She had been born a twin and was not expected to live. But she is a survivor and proved them wrong. She had a cerebral bleed that left her with severe Cerebral Palsy. She was in a wheelchair, cortically blind, primarily used her left side, struggled with bowel and bladder control, sucked her thumb incessantly, did not speak, had mostly baby teeth, a seizure disorder and a disproportionate, but beautiful, face.

Jesseye and I went to the library nearly every day while I was on the island. One day I noticed a flyer about Attention Deficit Hyperactivity Disorder (ADHD) on the bulletin board. I had worked with a number of people with ADHD so I was curious. I phoned the number and was even more interested after the conversation with someone at The HANDLE Institute. I couldn't make that presentation but there was another coming up called "Disgruntled with the Dys'es" on learning disabilities. That sounded equally interesting so I signed us up... Jessica too, as I was her only caregiver.

The first thing that happened when Jesseye and I walked in the door was that she and Judith Bluestone, the speaker, began communicating. This was amazing! Only family and those who had been around her a lot could communicate easily with Jesseye.

I must have looked silly with the grin that was plastered on my face as Judith said things like, "Children show us what they need," and "HANDLE looks for and treats the root cause of a problem." Yippee! Wahoo! Finally. I had, for too many years, been "treating" behaviors, rather than finding and treating the root cause of the behavior. It was something that had nagged at me and was part of the reason I was ready for a change.

Toward the end of her presentation, Judith asked Jesseye if she would help Judith with some demonstrations. She gave her permission and they were soon on the floor together. But Jesseye stiffened and was not able to do the intended exercise. Judith had an answer to that: joint tapping. Two therapists from other disciplines who were present became anxious that tapping would worsen her hypertonal state. But Judith reassured them that she was not going to tap on muscles, which would in fact have caused contractures. As the therapists continued to protest from their background based on neuromuscular activity, not on neurodevelopment... Surprise! Jesseye relaxed and was able to do the exercise Judith wanted to demonstrate.

I was so excited about what I had seen and heard that three weeks after returning home to Alaska, I went back to Seattle for my first introductory workshop. Within a matter of weeks, I had taken the advanced training as well, and immediately began some supervised clinical work in Seattle.

That was followed by Judith going to my town, Homer, Alaska.

Judith gave two talks and saw five children while in Homer. One of them was Freddie, a child with Fetal Alcohol Syndrome, with whom I had worked for years. One of the outcomes of Fetal Alcohol Syndrome is that these children often do not understand boundaries: social, emotional, physical. I will never forget the day that Freddie leaned within inches of my mother's face, studying her closely for many seconds, then asking, "Who crumpled your face?"

Freddie was twelve when Judith saw him in the spring of 1997. When he colored in a coloring book, he would use four or five colors, scribbling across the page until it turned black. He would jump into people's arms, wrapping his legs around them in greeting and had to be pried away. He nailed pieces of wood together randomly until they covered my entire shop floor in a giant work of "modern art." He swung pieces of stick about in play, having no idea that they may hit someone and hurt them. He did not understand about speaking softly or about ownership or personal space. Freddie had never drawn a human figure. Much of Freddie's HANDLE program had to do with understanding about his own body in space so that he could understand

A drawing by Freddie, age 12,
prior to his HANDLE evaluation and program.

about boundaries. He needed first to understand them in himself. The first sign that he began to "know" boundaries came when he colored Joan of Ark in a coloring book with five different colors, one for each part of the drawing, every one within the lines. Next a Respite Care Worker wanted to know what had happened; Freddie had shook her hand *and* let go after his greeting! Then, at Christmas time, Freddie presented his foster mother with a drawing: Santa Claus. He was fat with a round head, eyes, nose, mouth, a red hat with a little ball at the end, a coat, trousers, five fingers and five toes! Having worked with Freddie since he was four, he gave me the most wonderful gift when he said, "Cathy finally found what I need!"

Next came several months of following Judith around the country, working side by side and trying my hand at public presentations about HANDLE. What came next was pure privilege. Judith asked me to join her in England to help see clients and teach. I began to teach the introductory workshop and now I taught it in Europe. I had never before been out of North America!

The enthusiasm from Judith's previous visit and this visit generated an intense desire on the part of numerous people to begin advanced training and engage in an internship. Judith was much too busy in the U.S. to take on Europe to this extent, so the next thing I knew, I was chosen to teach the advanced training and to supervise the European internship program!

It has been five years since Jesseye and I had our wonderful five and a half weeks together. The following year I returned for another five and a half weeks. Jesseye had begun her HANDLE program just three weeks before I arrived. So she and I carried on while her family was away. We did activities to strengthen her vestibular system, Face Tapping, Crazy Straw, Peacemaker Massage, Hug and Tug, and a few more activities. She enjoyed our HANDLE time.

When her Mother walked in the door from their vacation she exclaimed, seemingly to the neighbors, "Jesseye look at your face, it has grown!" Indeed the side of Jesseye's face that had stopped growing had begun to grow again. "That's not all," I said. "Jesseye, open your mouth and show everyone." Jess opened and there were three new permanent teeth!

Today Jesseye uses both hands, can reach her arms above her head, has new permanent teeth. As for me, I have my own clinic in Homer, Alaska, and eight terrific interns studying with me there. I am still traveling overseas. I have been to seven countries, representing The HANDLE Institute from Scotland to South Africa. I have taught over two-dozen introductory classes and have supervised three batches of Interns from seven countries. I have met many wonderful people and learned so much from every one of them. And I have been privileged to watch as others carry on the work and see lives changed.

I am still excited about what I am doing and hope to share it with many others. I am ever grateful to Judith, her energy, her belief and her vision. And I am grateful to Jessica, because without her, I would not have found HANDLE!

"AND WHAT AM I? CHOPPED LIVER?"
FRANCES MEISER

Meeting Judith and her team at a HANDLE community presentation was like a light in the dark. At age 50, I was taking a variety of drugs and had, still, no real peace in my life. I believe, genuinely, that the ADHD and panic symptoms that I experienced throughout my school years resurfaced due to the hormonal changes of menopause. How devastating to be, once again, the hyperactive, disorganized child whom the teacher threatened to tie to her chair to keep her still. No threats this time, but with menopause, I was not in control of my own activity level and had difficulty organizing my thoughts.

Following the HANDLE presentation, I visited briefly with Judith and decided that I would make a trip from Austin to Seattle to attend a HANDLE workshop, *A Stitch in Time*. It was clear to me that I could use this information, at the very least, to help me help others—those who might otherwise be doomed, as I was, to suffering. I realized, immediately, the tremendous value of Judith's work for children with neurodevelopmental and nutritional challenges.

As some of the other class participants from Austin began planning how they might bring HANDLE to Texas, they ignored any contribution I made. As before, my peers were discounting me. But this time, I had the self-confidence to insist that I, too, be taken seriously as someone who could contribute to this work. In my question, "What am I?

Chopped Liver?" I released the frustration of so many years of being disregarded. And I decided to have my own HANDLE evaluation and exercises. And in this process, I realized the value this unique approach held for me too. I quickly began to notice substantial changes in how I experienced my world:

♦ I can shower with my eyes closed, without a sense of panic, and enjoy the feeling of water falling on my face.

♦ I can skip and hop and play patty-cake games. I can apply these activities to my teaching about the developmental needs of young children.

♦ I read more fluently.

♦ I sleep better.

♦ I see pictures in my brain. Having never before experienced such, I was ecstatic when a vision came to me one morning on awakening. I saw, in my mind, what I was going to do that day!

♦ I can spend time with family and friends, joyful time, quiet and tranquil.

♦ I am now the driver in my life; I have stopped feeling so driven.

After several more years of studying the HANDLE approach, I began to envision ways to get the very basics of Judith's work to children and parents. I wrote two books, one for children and one for adults, about the basics of caring for their brains: *The Brain Train* and *Senior Moments, Vanishing Thoughts: Causes and Remedies.* This spring, I completed my M.Ed. in Language and Literacy from an Austin university. I know, without question, that I could not have accomplished this without the help of Judith and the HANDLE approach.

Now, at 58 years old, I do just a few HANDLE exercises—to keep me "tuned-up." But, in times of high stress, I return to my full HANDLE program and pay close attention to my diet and rest. My ability to navigate through life's challenges has greatly improved.

I sing the praises of the HANDLE approach whenever and wherever I can. My wish is for the educational community to see, soon, that HANDLE has the potential to change the world of education; to begin to meet the needs of the millions of children that are now left behind due to their own neurodevelopmental challenges.

I know that my personal disillusionment with the world came from within, but once resolved, I began to experience the joy and wonder of life all around me. When I work with a child who has ADHD, I can truthfully say, "I know how you feel inside and the stress you are experiencing. But I can help you move beyond the stress to experience life with intense joy, in a relaxed way, and with the knowledge that you can achieve what you desire."

Yes, Virginia, there is a Santa Claus and it is Judith Bluestone. She has a bag full of gifts for all of us and it is there for the asking!

OF PERSEVERANCE AND HOPE
KATE BOWERS

Nestled into my little cabin in the woods, a brisk fire crackling away, I settle into my favorite window seat, hands warming on a cup of tea, and I contemplate how I'll construct a set of music for a small music festival I'll play next month. My mind wanders to the yoga class I'll teach next summer—my small contribution to a visionary project which inspires people from all over the country to reach beyond themselves to others, transforming themselves in the process. Within the next year, I hope to open our educational camp—the inception of a wondrous woodsy haven for those who share an interest in making the world a better place.

This story, about the unraveling and remaking of my life, starts 46 years ago. In my earliest memories, I made the acquaintance of cows and buttercups, and played in an apple orchard with an imaginary snapping turtle that lived in a pit under the railroad tracks. I spent free days that seemed to last forever, roaming and exploring seasonal wonders. I loved sunshine, bugs, running, cows and making bowls full of bubbles. Then I started kindergarten. The days were long. I wanted to be home. My family moved three times that year.

First grade presented my first big problem. We were learning to read but everything was getting tangled up. The lines would seem to move; I'd lose my place, get all confused. When I tried to write, I couldn't figure out which way the letters were supposed to go. The class divided into groups and I went with the kids that couldn't learn that well. That was embarrassing. I didn't get much attention. I hardly ever spoke to anybody.

By second grade, I tried to stay in the back of the classroom, hoping nobody would notice me. I had a hard time following what the teacher said, got bored and sometimes just stared out the window until the teacher called on me, and then I embarrassed myself by acting confused. School began to feel like torment.

Reading eluded me through second, third and into fourth grade. An optometrist around the corner tested my eyes, and then gave me a screen to put over the TV. He told me I was to wear special glasses to watch television. When my eye wandered, a big black strip would appear on the TV screen, making it impossible to see. After a while, I wore the glasses less and less and soon no one harped at me about it anymore. There were eye exercises too, but since nobody cared if I did them, I also stopped those.

At school there was a problem much more pressing than eye exercises or reading. Diane, a girl who'd been held back five years and was well into puberty in third grade, decided I was her number one choice for self-esteem building through abuse of the weak and the frail. Not every day, but with sickening frequency, I stood face to face with Diane, who loved to launch a fist into my solar plexus and run away laughing.

Avoiding bullies and making sense of the work were my chief occupations at school. Finally, a fifth grade teacher realized that if he instructed me again, after the class got to work, that I could do considerably better. With Mr. Sloan's assistance, I moved up from the bottom math group to the top. At last, some small success at school. It felt good, but it was my last for a long time.

At home, I heralded little attention and kept my problems to myself. Home life was raucous. I sought quiet. When forced indoors, I climbed onto the high shelf in my parent's clothes closet to escape the noise. The closet offered a hidden pocket of peace and solitude. On Saturdays, I ran away, straight to the woods, to smell the mud, splash in the river and stare at the sky.

Seventh grade, in a new school, in a new town, drove home the reality of the poverty our family was experiencing. Grim days those were for Midwest manufacturing industries. I watched my father send out resumes, then hold his head in his hands as he encountered rejection after rejection. The temperature dropped. The money ran out. The heat was turned off in October. My mother showed signs of unraveling. My brother seethed. Feelings of panic grew inside all of us. I felt myself to be a burden.

One day, in the schoolyard, I was stalked. My latest rival, Sherry, was a bully par excellence. My name had been connected, behind hands shielding whispers, with rumors of betrayal of one of the girls. A judgment of guilty was rendered upon the innocent. While walking home, I crossed the overpass, was ambushed and trapped by a group of ten girls, taunting me as they circled. Sherry stepped into the center of the circle, and within inches of me, began screaming. The realization of what was happening, the potential danger, and the fact that I was trapped left me suddenly strangely detached. It occurred to me that my only option was to sit, cover my head, and pray. Which I did. The girls kicked, they punched, they pressed my skull into the concrete and called me terrible names. Bored with my passivity, they eventually wandered off. The next day I ached all over, was covered with bruises and could barely move.

Once, a group of younger children jumped me as I walked home from school. They pulled me down, climbed all over me and pounded my head into the sidewalk. Another attack involved a rape orchestrated by both girls and boys. I feared I was pregnant. I became too agitated to sleep at night; I could not eat. I tried to cope with fear and the growing cold by experimenting with relaxing my body from my toes to my head. It helped. I experienced leaving my body and looking down from above at my figure reclining there on the bed.

By eighth grade, I was regularly skipping school. It was easy to get a note from my father, so I just stayed home. On one occasion, I couldn't remember which day I needed a note for, so I asked my father to write, "Please excuse Kate for the day she was absent." Then he signed it. I found carbon paper in the bedroom closet left over from the old woman who had died in my room. Very early in the morning, while the others slept, I made carbon copies of the note my father had written, and soon I had a good stack of excuses to use anytime I needed.

One day, when I made a rare visit to the other eighth

graders at school, I was called into the principal's office. "Somebody saw you on the streets last week and why are you never in school?" the principal interrogated, staring me down. I remained silent. He pointed to a display of papers on his desk. There, lined in neat rows, were my carefully carbon copied excuses in rows five across and deep. There was a funny look on his face and I, knowing I was caught, could only smile. I was reprimanded and warned of being expelled and I never went back. Instead, I wandered the streets after sleeping in late, when it was warmest, and dreamed of running away.

The year I was thirteen, I lost the capacity to cry. The year I was fourteen, dry eyed and numbed from too much pain, I left home, swearing that if I survived I would remember children and gentle souls trampled in a brutal downward spiral.

The Greyhound bus dropped me in Chicago, a place unlike any other I had seen. By September, I had an apartment with roommates, and worked five nights at an ice cream parlor. I enrolled in high school, using a bit of chicanery to do so.

Mornings were torment. I tried to get up early enough so I could walk the few miles to school. I felt disoriented and heavy when I awoke, as if I'd been drugged. I arrived at school nauseated and faint. My attendance failed. The teachers never questioned my self-written and signed excuses. When I signed my own report cards, using my own name, school administrators did not question me. I lied to roommates about my age and whereabouts during the day; they would be unlikely to harbor a runaway. A couple of months later I got my starting time at the ice cream parlor confused and came in late. I was fired on the spot.

I continued to find jobs because I developed street smarts, but I found it difficult to keep them. The reasons given for being fired varied: incorrect math, spilling and dropping, failing to carry out verbal instructions, slowness, lack of organization, etc. I attributed the job failures to youth, lack of education and to my personal weaknesses. It wasn't until I was reading Dickens and studying about the roots of poverty, that I began to understand that I was part of a vast web of greater suffering. Growing knowledge of the persistence, and the scale and depth of human suffering lodged in my soul.

Despite the frequent firings, the jobs I found sustained

me while they lasted. Eventually, I began working in night-clubs along the sizzling musical strip on Chicago's north side. Music embedded itself deeply into my life. In the Chicago folk scene, I heard songs that spoke of feelings deep in my heart that I could not express. I found beautiful acoustic sounds that mesmerized and soothed my tormented heart.

At last, and with a deep sense of relief, I turned eighteen. Through several turns of fate, I wound up living in San Francisco. Finally, I had a chance to reflect on where I'd been, and to realize the deep emotional and physical scars sustained in those difficult years. My breathing became short and I had difficulty completing a sentence. I ached inside, but could not cry. I began binge eating. I felt that I drifted through life as though in a fog. I developed headaches around my eyes that never went away. I feared a brain tumor. I had waited years for a spot in the current of life that was calm and when I finally found it, I discovered how much turmoil remained inside, and that there would be no true rest until I rid myself of the residual bitterness that clung to me from the hunger, privation and violence of my early years.

Scouting around, I found a therapist who was highly regarded with respect to children's issues. I was then working full-time as a housekeeper and cook for a residential treatment home for people with autism. Seeing the therapist took a big bite of my income. The expense was tough, but I knew I couldn't heal myself alone. One day the therapist announced that he had fallen in love with me, though he was married, and that in order for me to advance in therapy, we would have to reconcile this issue. I knew just how to reconcile this issue, and lots more cheaply than the therapist had in mind. I walked out and never looked back.

I looked again for a therapist; this time a woman. The day of my appointment arrived and I, excited and nervous, got the time wrong, and got there with almost two hours to spare. I wandered around and found a yoga school nearby. A class was scheduled to start right away, so I took it. In that first yoga class, sadness welled up inside from regions deep within, sadness inexpressible within the realm of words. Sadness trapped in my muscles, breath and seemingly, in my very cells.

The class finished and I walked across the street to my appointment with the therapist. I walked in, sat down and broke into sobs that lasted for a very long while. The therapist, astonished, silently held me and stayed with me until the sobs dwindled. Warmth swept through me as I felt a deep release within. Those tears, so long repressed, washed deep sadness from my soul.

Rather than returning to the therapist, I returned to yoga, and with that began the work of healing heart and soul. I fell deeply into yoga. I lived a quiet, contemplative life of yoga, meditation, vegan diet and abundant solitude aside from my work with autistic children. This lasted for several years, until I decided it was time to go to college.

I began on my way to filling in the large blanks that had been left when I assiduously avoided school. I began acquiring a vocabulary less redolent of street life and more acceptable to middle class sensibilities. I studied long and hard, passed my GED with flying colors, was awarded a scholarship and received college financial assistance as a destitute minority. Things were looking up.

College did pose problems. I had a very difficult time reading schedules and finding classes. I had no idea how to write or how to speak to college professors without offending them. I had difficulty keeping my mind on reading, on homework. The problem, I decided, was mental discipline. Because it was like math but more fun, I opted to major in music—for mental discipline.

The classroom lights were excessively bright for me, so I took to wearing caps. My reception in the music department ranged from derision to open hostility. One exasperated teacher explained that they didn't want students in the music department to learn music; they wanted musicians already developed, to use music school to hone their craft. I refused to be cowed or run. I'd decided it was music that would organize my brain—somehow. I struggled and barely held on for four years.

I worked full-time through school and seldom had a moment to reflect on life. I continued getting fired from jobs. I struggled for years after college with every job I had. I felt confusion, fear, anxiety, slowness, inefficiency. I started feeling deeply insecure about myself and my ability to rise above my circumstances. Years passed. After being fired yet again, I sought the help of a neurologist who diagnosed me with a right brain learning disability. Receiving no more information than that, this became a time of deep sadness as I realized that I had yet to wrestle a very powerful demon—my own mind.

A psychiatrist diagnosed me with Attention Deficit Disorder (ADD) and offered to prescribe Ritalin. I checked with a drug counselor and learned that Ritalin has the potential to trigger clinical depression. When I presented this drawback to the psychiatrist, he offered to prescribe for that too. I declined drugs and maintained my yoga practice. The yoga was extremely beneficial, yet it failed to provide an efficacious means to resolve the underlying causes and the manifestations of my brain's apparent quirks.

For years, I gnawed on the notion that people have various and distinct learning profiles—some that are quite unique and in direct conflict with traditional teaching methods. Because our system of education does not acknowledge this, otherwise bright students often fall into the dismal land of failure.

Over time, and through a series of seriously painful events, I realized something about myself regarding my own quirks. The signs followed me always. It's interesting, really, to consider having a neurological impairment, know it intuitively, yet have no language, no vernacular, no words to explain, or even ask about the quirks.

My quirks were often subtle, and varied in span, intensity, combination and in their ability to hamper my productive activity. They included squinting in the sunlight and being bothered by bright light and loud sounds. Crazy things like saying the wrong word. Or forgetting words. Hearing things all wrong. Losing things. Bumping into things. And getting lost. Anywhere. Everywhere. Always.

I couldn't follow verbal directions. If other voices were audible in the background, I couldn't even follow conversation. I had difficulty getting my eyes to focus, and couldn't see properly if I was looking through binoculars; I saw two things, not one. My skin rebelled at all kinds of fabrics and tight clothing. Something was wrong, a bit wacky, and it caused hardship.

Books recommended time management, exercise and rigid adherence to schedules. I wondered aloud, to an optometrist, if my wandering, divergent eyes had anything to do with learning disabilities. He said no. I visited medical libraries and bookstores, looking for ways to rectify the quirks. Finally, years later, Judith Bluestone's work—her holistic approach that viewed the body's various systems in unity—provided me with answers to the source of my problems and solutions that I had spent years trying to find.

When I met Cathy Stingley, in Homer Alaska, she supplied a large piece of the puzzle, bringing order to my own life—and to the world around me, as I perceived it. While in Homer, I allowed Cathy to perform a HANDLE evaluation on me, as part of her HANDLE internship. The evaluation was eye opening, confirming what the neurologist's evaluation had presented. But, I must admit, the exercises taught to me seemed a bit silly. They were also somewhat demanding, and to me, a little confusing, so I abandoned them.

Thinking I might like to teach special education led me to work in a special education department with an autistic teen named Russell. No one had ever spoken to Russell about his autism; instead, they talked around him, and about him, as though he were non-existent. I assumed, despite his difficulties with verbal expression, that he understood quite a bit. We began engaging in conversation; I asked yes/no questions about what it was he wanted. Armed with Russell's answers, we set about learning what we could about autism from the writings of Temple Grandin. We used what we learned to form a visual presentation of autism from Russell's point of view. The presentation became very popular in the school district and beyond; we gave over forty talks in one year.

While I was working with Russell, the teacher of a contained special education classroom let me create a HANDLE program for six high-school students with a range of developmental disabilities, including autism. Within this group, even the teacher had difficulties. Generally, she jumbled her words in such a manner that set the cart before the horse—leading to confusion. (Judith calls this "verbal cluttering.") As a HANDLE intern, and knowing my limitations regarding HANDLE techniques, I was pleased with the opportunity to practice.

The children were drawn to the activities, and would practice at home on their own. We asked one high functioning student to "help" so that she would get in the therapeutic activities that she needed without diminishing her self-image. And as she helped others, she reported that writing and spelling became easier. Within a couple of months, there was improvement all around—but the most startling was the teacher. She started speaking in clear, sequentially correct sentences!

Outside of our contained classroom, well intended special education teachers were closed to a perspective on Judith's work, believing instead that success was a matter of motivation. They continued teaching from a behavioral model and I watched as children were failed for things I knew they had no control over. In some, anger was palpable. Others kept trying and trying—to no avail. Very little progress was made. I realized that if I wanted to work in special education, I would have to work outside of the system.

Slowly, painfully, Russell developed rudimentary speech, by finding connections between what he saw and that seemingly incomprehensible world the world of words. Russell labored heroically, day in and out, to discover those connections. To me, Russell's struggle is an inspiring example of the beauty and strength of the human spirit to triumph against great odds.

The holistic approach—the systems method of HANDLE—plus respect for the client, nonjudgmental assessment and gentle enhancement, offered a sensible program. Now I incorporate much of Judith's work into my life, and into the classes I teach, particularly the yoga and voice classes. Seniors without the strength required for yoga balance poses find HANDLE techniques improve their balance. Voice students without strong rhythm respond to HANDLE techniques with gratitude. I perform noticeably better if I run through integrating HANDLE activities prior to a musical performance.

Finding ways to help other quirky ones through HANDLE practices is a dear pursuit for me, as is presenting yoga as a powerful tool for self-healing, and music as salve for the soul. They all blend in me now, providing wisdom. Answers to share with others. Over the years, I had learned to eliminate many pieces of life that caused pain because they aggravated my quirks. As I came to accept myself, I saw that with my quirks came qualities that made me special. I am creative and empathic. I can be highly focused and look upon the world in synergistic ways.

Gestures of faith, hope and kindness, large or small, sustained me in my darkest hours. My hope now is to be a shining light for others. In that spirit, I humbly offer this, a story of perseverance and hope. The great sustaining force for hope in those dark days was then, is now, and always will be loving kindness and, in HANDLE terms, gentle enhancement.

Above: Kate.

Right:
Welcome to Kate's.

Above: Kate's woodsy world; her place of
respite and peace in all seasons.

Postscript: "If you meet Kate Bowers at a yoga class, you will immediately be impressed with her enormous kindness. She positively radiates welcome and acceptance of all who come. Perhaps the most striking thing about her is her voice—deep and full, warm and calming. Kate walks you through the mysteries of yoga, holding you in the palm of her hand with her voice.

However, if you think that is Kate, hold onto your hats. When you meet Kate at the Bowers' retreat, thirty acres of woods and streams in the foothills of the Cascade Mountains in Washington, you are met with laughter and a serious risk of a practical joke. You may find your bed is short-sheeted or your shoes have disappeared; she definitely cheats at cards.

Then again, you can climb into the hot tub on a moonlit night and talk with Kate until the stars come out. There you will meet the Kate whose compassion extends to all the world and back again—to you."

—Margery Hite

BLOOD-BROTHER OF A TORTOISE
ELIZABETH MEYER

"In the High and Far-Off Times the Elephant, O Best Beloved, had no trunk." Rudyard Kipling tells the story of an Elephant Child who was full of "'satiable curtiosity"—which meant he asked ever so many questions. And because he was a little different, he was spanked by his mother and spanked by his father and spanked by all his many aunts and uncles.

So it was in my childhood, because I was "different," and an irritation to all my teachers, a temptation to tease (or worse) for other children, and constantly searching for approval. I was called "promising," but failed to live up to expectations.

I could never tell a story, because I stumbled over the words. I could read words—and read aloud very well—but not understand or remember what I had read. Standing to answer a question in class, everyone would laugh because I could not say anything. (When I was six or seven, anger and humiliation made me vengeful and I once stole a beautiful gold fountain pen. No one found out, but the anxiety stopped me from repeating that little exercise.) Later, my inability to read meant that I was limited in the subjects I could learn at school: no English Literature, Geography or History. I never touched a newspaper or journal. I had no general knowledge, no idea about current affairs. People would say in exasperation, "Don't you even know that?"

I was conscious of experiencing visual difficulties, but

nothing ever showed up in eye tests. School became more and more tiring as the reading became more demanding. Once or twice each term I would run a fever and sleep for three days, then start again. The tiredness was accompanied by frequent headaches and almost constant nausea. I was always pale and lacked initiative, too tired to follow my own interests or even to have time for friends. I was so slow that one of my teachers called me "the blood-brother of a tortoise."

At University, it became ever harder to keep up. Any time spent, other than working at my studies, I paid for dearly in terms of poor results. Depression and a sense of failure are my overriding memories. I simply did not understand how the other students managed so much better. They lived active lives, went out with friends until all hours, and had plenty of interests outside of their studies. Many had jobs in the vacations while I had to work every day to complete essays and prepare for the next term. My co-students were perfectly friendly, but I have to admit I minded that I could not share their better life at a college which had so much to offer.

My writing was a problem, and so untidy that often I could not read it myself. When I was about 11 years old, a dear friend of my father told me it was extremely rude to write illegibly, so I set about improving my writing by practising every day after I came home from school. At interview, after a University entrance exam, the tutor mentioned that I had made a number of "howlers," and that it would be a good idea if I re-read my papers before handing them in. I knew it would not help, but that was my secret.

At a time when sport played a major role in English schools, there was a terrible feeling of isolation for anyone so hopeless at sport, and especially ball games. Without a sense of balance, I fell frequently. On one occasion, when my mother picked me up, I screamed because I was convinced she was holding me upside-down. How confused and ashamed I felt when I opened my eyes! Later the lack of balance made me refuse ever to go for walks in company, because I was ashamed that I had to pause after every turn, every stile, until my balance caught up with me. This went on until I was 55.

Having neither sense of time nor direction, it was extremely difficult to find my way, leading me frequently to tears of frustration and being late for or missing appointments. Towns with one-way streets were a nightmare because I could not go back the way I had come. When I was driving with my sons in the car, it upset them too. The family came to say, "We'll expect you when we see you."

After my graduation in Biochemistry, I accepted a job as a technician at Brussels University, determined at that time never again to put myself into a position of having to take an exam. After a year, I was persuaded to embark on a Ph.D. It took me six years to complete, the whole last year spent just writing it up. In the end, I was successful but so exhausted that I could not do any serious work for another two years.

The time came when I wished to return to Britain. I had three interviews. Edinburgh University commented on my Third Class degree from Oxford, and said it was clear I had a poor basic knowledge. They could offer me a small teaching post. Harwell on the other hand looked at my Ph.D. and offered me the leadership of a group researching the effects of X-radiation on tissues. It sounded a wonderful job, but I knew I could never keep up with the journals and it would be a non-starter. I had to turn it down despite recognising what an opportunity they were giving me (including a most tempting salary!) The third was a position in cancer research in Glasgow, where it was agreed with the professor that my contribution would be mainly practical. There, I admitted that I found it hard to read the journals. I had one happy year there before financial constraints forced the director to require annual publications from each researcher; the miseries began again. I was threatened with loss of the job anyway because my depression became so severe that my work suffered. My weekly visits to a psychiatrist never made any significant impact on the depression. I had taken on a mortgage and could not walk away without a job.

The first help came with my discovery of a teacher of the Alexander Technique. It gave me considerable relief, and I decided to give up my house and go to London to train as an Alexander teacher myself. I had not been long on the course before the inability to read proved a major handicap.

In 1976, I married. My new training was interrupted by three months in hospital before the birth of our first son, Edward. I was not able to return to it. After two years, we had another son, James, and though I had desperately wanted children, the reality was something else. My mother had two relevant quotations: "'Have it', said God. 'Have it and pay for it!'" I paid dearly in exhaustion and depression. "There are two important things in life: the first to know what you want, the second to want it when you have it." The change to becoming a housewife and mother at 42, with all its restrictions, was almost intolerable. I was unable to organise my life, the mess in the house spiralled out of control, and I did not know how to manage.

At five years old, Edward went to the local school, where he was clearly unhappy. We used to see him, pale and alone, in a corner of the playground as far from everyone else as he could be. (At home, he would beat up his brother if James so much as put on music. We were later to discover he was hypersensitive to sound.) He was bored in class. Reading was easy for him. He had taught himself long before school, from reading newspapers and playing with letters. Writing was a different matter; he could not write more than a few lines per day. He had learned to work out the ages of people from the dates on tombstones in our local cemetery round the village kirk. At school, they were working in single or double figures.

Generally, Edward was a quiet and compliant child. In the evening, he would read grown-up books with my mother, because I could not admit they were too difficult for me. It is uncomfortable to find your five year-old is so much more able than you are. It was only much later that I understood that, like me, he started to read early, but comprehension difficulties set in with more demanding, independent reading.

James joined Edward at school two years later. An indomitably cheerful child at the start, he experimented one day with a first class tantrum. He terrified the teacher and he knew it; thereafter she had no control over him. He charmed with his smile, went walk-about and did his own thing. He refused to read, though his teacher told me his reading was "age-appropriate." He was 11 before I understood he really could not read.

Both boys went to my husband's old Prep School, because he had been so happy there. When James was eight, I had to write to both boys that their father was critically ill. The Headmaster said James had been uninterested. What I heard later from the matron was that in the middle of the night James had sought her out and asked her to read the letter to him. In fact, he was well into his teens before he could read handwriting.

I took James to Peter Blythe at the Institute for Neuro-Physiological Psychology in Chester. When I saw his assessment, I realised I had comparable problems. Peter gave James and me each a neuro-developmental programme.

Edward had moved on by then, to secondary school. I had been concerned about Edward because I had seen in him so many things I remembered from my childhood: the need to work without distraction to keep up good results, the tiredness and pallor, the food intolerances, his difficulty with sports, the lack of friends. The first time he took an interest in theatre lighting for the school play, which involved taking time for rehearsals, his work results plummeted. When I explained Peter's findings to him, he wanted an assessment too. He also started a programme. An early touching comment, Edward said, "At last I have time to talk to people." Not even I, his mother, had realised how hard he worked.

The brighter the child, the more difficult it is for teachers to comprehend that they can have specific learning difficulties. Though Edward was helped by Peter's program, he never felt he would be believed that he still had problems. Only after he failed second year at University could we persuade him to go to learning support. Then, in January 1999, he had a HANDLE assessment, and he started his HANDLE programme. HANDLE has truly transformed his life. Within five days of starting, he told me that writing was easier. He is reading with improved comprehension.

Edward is currently doing sound therapy to reduce his hypersensitivity. His newfound stamina and enjoyment of life are a delight to witness, and his sporting activities, individual and team play, are hugely improved. He has gone on to a second University degree and we feel he now leads a happily balanced life of work and play, performing competently and efficiently. He was the top student of his group last year.

For me starting Peter Blythe's programme in 1991 was quite an experience. Peter himself had reservations about letting me do it, but I insisted I could not carry on the way I was. After four terrible months where I lost my compensation strategies, improvements became evident. Gradually, I felt more able to live. Laughter came into our home, I could enjoy my children, had time to do things with them. I could walk in company without being afraid of the stiles and

turns. Instead of having eyes glued to the ground for security, I could enjoy the lovely country around us, the fantastic skies and light play of the Scottish hills, the sun glisten-
ing on the raindrops on each pine needle. There was time
for friends and outside activities.

Peter trained me in his reflex inhibition programme, and
inspired me to look beyond it at other therapies such as a
variety of Sound Therapies, craniosacral therapy, and in
1998, we had the first seminar on the HANDLE approach.
That seminar was another revelation. My reading ability
and comprehension were still not good, I was hypersensitive
to smell, touch, light and sound, and booked an assessment for the earliest opportunity. For ten months, I carried
my programme through daily, and then added sound therapy, which helped to improve my listening and understanding against background noise.

The result is that I can now read for pleasure, I have an
idea of current affairs, and my dream of working in the field
of learning difficulty therapies is coming true. I have become a HANDLE intern and I have set up my own little cen-
tre. My colleague, a craniosacral therapist and Feldenkrais
practitioner, who works with me one to two days a week, is
also a HANDLE intern. We want to combine our various
trainings to give our clients the best individual help we
know.

The Elephant Child's "'satiable curtiosity" was stilled by
the Kolokolo bird's suggestion, "Go to the banks of the great
grey-green greasy Limpopo river, all set about with fever
trees," to find out what the Crocodile has for dinner. Peter
Blythe has been my Kolokolo bird, constructively guiding
me and encouraging me at every stage, most recently towards HANDLE. I am deeply grateful.

After the Bi-Coloured-Python-Rock-Snake had rescued
The Elephant Child with his new trunk, he says, "You
couldn't have done *that* with a mere-smear nose." Like to
the Elephant Child, my brother-in-law keeps saying to me,
"You could not have done *that* before..." Every intervention
has been like another tug by the crocodile on the nose of
the elephant. The new sense of "Yes I *can*" is much appreciated. Like the Elephant Child, I say, "Thank you" to Judith for the excellent extension to the "trunk."

INDEFATIGABLE RESOLVE
A POSTSCRIPT BY JUDITH BLUESTONE

Frances and Kate and Elizabeth each, in their own way, suffered immeasurable pain due to inefficiencies in their neurological functioning. How exhausting, and how devastating to the psyche, to know that you should be able to do something, are expected to do it, only to discover that you can't, no matter how hard you try. You can imagine yourself doing it, as Kate in a field of buttercups and snapping turtles, but you can't organize yourself sufficiently to bring it to fruition. When the "it" is academic learning, or ease in social situations, the failure pervades deeply into psychological realms. Insecurity, poor self-esteem, depression, anger—these are all rational responses to the irrational situation caused by neurological inefficiencies.

And how disheartening to seek help and find none. Or to find help that serves only to mask your problems, and in so doing, thwarts your talents. Or help focused narrowly on the outcome, neglecting the human spirit that must move in synchrony as a whole—body-mind-spirit—toward goals that extend far beyond a spelling test or standardized exam. How fortunate when those providing some help realize that their guidance provides only a limited answer, and guide the weary and desperate to explore other plausible options that might resolve the roots of their challenges.

These women and their journeys are remarkable. With their inefficiencies, they've exhausted themselves, and at times, those around them. Yet each persisted, to survive and to achieve, despite how they were reflected by others—others without an understanding of the torment. Their success, survival even, is a result of, and a tribute to, their indefatigable resolve.

These women and their journeys are inspirational. Yet, those weaker of spirit continue suffering without respite as they succumb to frustration, experience chronic fatigue or engage in outbursts of rage against the backdrop of their systems' inefficiencies. Only with a unity of purpose, and efficient, synchronous functionality, comes ability.

Looking solely at the injured parts, or solely at the healthy parts—neither provides the answer. Only when you can see the whole, realize the synchrony, and understand what the aberrant behaviors are telling you—which systems need to be strengthened, and which need to be integrated—can you achieve flexible and resilient functionality.

Because HANDLE works on just such a holistic basis to increase efficiency, even those with severe brain injury have found help. Through the Gentle Enhancement of weak systems and an understanding of the principles of neural plasticity throughout the lifespan, HANDLE continues to prove that the body can help reintegrate the brain, even years after injury. What areas of the brain respond? Different areas, depending on the constellation of strengths and weaknesses, functionality and dysfunctionality, that the person demonstrates today and that were part of that person's developmental history. Our problems rarely spring into bloom from nowhere. They are usually rooted in our past inefficiencies and our recent traumas, combined.

Looking only at the distant past or at the recent events does not yield solutions. We are whole and our histories are whole. Those who know this move beyond momentary trials to lasting triumph. And they do this not for themselves, but for the whole system—community of the world—of which they are an integral part.

PART 2

IT DEPENDS ON HOW YOU LOOK AT THINGS

—Ben Ross Berenberg
The Churkendoose
Part Chicken, Turkey, Duck and Goose

FOCUSING

A PREFACE BY CATHY STINGLEY, CERTIFIED HANDLE PRACTITIONER

Our town is small, about 4,000 people. Sally Oberstein, a lively, animated, highly active member of the community dropped out of sight one day. Even close friends did not know what had happened to her.

Slowly, after months, Sally began to reappear. She used a walker at first and was only seen briefly. Later I saw her at live performances in our theater. I had heard a little about her difficulties. "Something about balance or the inner ear," people would say.

There were many who suggested I should contact Sally to tell her about HANDLE. When I first started as a HANDLE practitioner, excited and enthusiastic about what I was doing, I tried contacting members of the community whom I felt could benefit from HANDLE. However, people were not ready to hear, and certainly not from someone saying they had one more thing that might make a difference.

Later, I asked Sally if she would have come to see me if I had approached her. Her answer was simple. "No." I have learned that people need to hear about something new from three sources. Sally says she heard about HANDLE, and about me, for over a year. She had also heard about other things, and had tried some of them with little or no success, so she was leery of trying yet another thing.

Each time I saw Sally at the theater she would walk in with someone and receive help being seated. But her vulnerability became plainly obvious when the show was over. Two people were needed to hold her on either side and guide her out of the theater into the common area and out to the car. It was like watching a very old lady. From my HANDLE perspective, I surmised that the lighting changes, movement across the stage, gestures of the actors, being in the dark, and moving her head to watch the program all combined to impact on the vestibular system within her inner ear, stressing it to the point of literally shutting down by the end of the program.

When she finally decided to come see me, two years after the surgery that compromised her equilibrium, Sally drove herself to my house and walked from the car slowly, using a single cane. Although she drove, moving her head to look in both directions was very disorienting. Driving up hill made her dizzy. Walking downstairs or downhill was extremely difficult. She had most recently been a dancer, writer, jeweler, singer and traveler. Aside from making short entries in her journal, she was unable to do any of these. She wanted desperately to be physically active again.

Sally has long, dark, beautiful hair. To comb it caused dizziness, nausea and disorientation. Generally congenial and pleasant, she would disappoint herself with angry outbursts at people who moved carelessly around her, threatening her precarious balance. She wanted to be able to go into a crowded room without feeling anxiety and without feeling alone. Getting to sleep and staying asleep were very difficult. She wanted to go to the theater and walk out normally. She described her body as that of an old lady, no longer agile and barely mobile. Sally observed that she would forget things easily and needed me to write down the high points of our visit so she could remember them. Still she would forget them.

When she began her HANDLE program, Sally did her vestibular exercises seated in a chair. These are usually done on the floor with full body movement from side to side, front to back and rolling. Sally sat exceedingly still and would tip her head toward one shoulder about fifteen degrees, then upright, then toward the other shoulder. She would tip her head forward almost imperceptibly, bring it upright and *begin* the movement to tip it back. That was it for one day!

Sally did a number of things to re-learn her own body

and where it was in space, since her vestibular system was not giving her reliable information. Among these were eyes-closed activities, at first while seated. Many months into her program she reported with great enthusiasm that she had done one of her exercises in the shower. She'd done a half turn with her eyes closed, a true triumph.

With my (HANDLE's) guidance, Sally worked to move her eyes and her head without losing her balance and becoming nauseated and disoriented. She practiced conversations with background noise. She learned activities to help her multi-task again and to strengthen her memory. She used supplements to help support her new functioning. She wore leotards to give her more information about where her body was in space.

Ten months after beginning her HANDLE program, Sally decided to try taking the 16-hour HANDLE introductory workshop. She was in a room with ten other people. By now she had shed her cane. Walking in, she looked like any other member of the class. However, she sat under bright light in an otherwise dimly lit room, facing me with her "good" ear. During early introductions, Sally shared some of her story with the class, so they were aware of her sensitivities.

About 45 minutes into class one night, I stopped and asked Sally if she would share with the group what was happening with her at that moment. She was seated at the corner of a table, her legs spread wide and feet flat on the floor. She clung almost white-knuckled to the edges of the table, her eyes were closed and her skin was pale.

With a sheepish grin, Sally explained that when she walked into the room that night she smelled hot chocolate. She just could not resist and, knowing what would happen, made herself a cup. She explained that since the surgery, the chemistry of her inner ear was very fragile; that sugar, caffeine, alcohol, salt, MSG and not enough water would quickly affect her balance, ability to focus, attend and use more than one sense at a time, and her awareness of her body in space. She could lose her balance and become nauseated. Hence, her broad stance gave her stability, her hands kept her from falling from the chair, and closing her eyes allowed her to continue to listen to what I was saying without being visually overwhelmed by my gestures and movement. But the hot chocolate tasted great!

Sally worked her way up to doing the vestibular exercises on the floor and with several repetitions. She finds dropping her head to her shoulder somewhat difficult and avoids sudden, fast movement. She watches her diet. Sally is now much more comfortable in a crowded place, though not one hundred percent.

It is still difficult for her to carry on a conversation in a noisy environment, but she is capable of it. If the cordless phone has not been put back in its cradle, she cannot find it if it is ringing, since she has not regained the ability to echolocate. If her son calls for her to come to him from another part of the house, he must tell her where he is, as she cannot determine where his voice is coming from. However, Sally can now dance, ride a bike, sing (however difficult with the loss of half of her hearing), do jewelry work, manage a new, successful, full-time business, and, obviously (as you will see from the story that follows), write. She can walk forward and backward with her eyes closed, drive uphill without getting dizzy, move about in the dark, go downstairs and downhill, and lift heavy objects. She says, "I can move!" If you met Sally today, you would not know there was anything wrong with her.

FOCUSING
SALLY OBERSTEIN

I tried to see the nurse in front of me but when I opened my eyes, everything spun so fast that I threw up. I threw up over and over. The room sped past as if I were riding a cross-country train. The picture of a sterile room with gray linoleum, a television mounted high on a shelf, the large round clock against a beige wall, only came into focus when I closed my eyes. 11:15.

I didn't belong in a hospital. I just drifted in a dug-out canoe down a murky tributary of the Amazon, watching toucans and parrots soar from tree to tree. I just trekked the hill country of Thailand and snorkeled the Great Barrier Reef. I was just married in Italy on a miniscule island west of Capri, and honeymooned in Positano with cobblestone passages to the beach, where the cool March air carried smells of fish from brightly painted dories. My new husband and I hiked up a hillside to a tiny white-washed village, sat on a cliff and ate fresh bread with cheese and red ripe tomatoes, watching the green Mediterranean Sea below.

Green scrubs. The nurses wore green uniforms. I argued with one with my eyes closed. "Whatever you're giving me in my I.V. is making me feel sick."

"The I.V. is making you feel better," she said.

"It's not working," I complained as she left the room.

I lifted the gauze bandage to uncover my right ear and could hear the ticking of the big clock. It was the same clock on the wall in Mr. Sapp's fifth-grade classroom. Tick, then a pause, then a tick. I could barely wait to leave for school each morning. He couldn't still be teaching. It's been thirty-three years. Tick...pause...tick.

I peeked out at spinning beige and brown, and threw up into a sterile plastic blue bowl. The sheets were sterile. The smell was sterile. I wondered what made that sterile smell. Was it alcohol? Floor cleaner? I forgot to ask. I looked at the big clock and quickly closed my eyes again. 11:18! I wanted out. Not out of the hospital to the chilly fall air of Anchorage, Alaska, but out of my body that failed to recover, failed to let me see straight and get out of bed. I wanted to crawl out of my skin. I shook my head, which made me sick again.

More sterile blue bowls, more green scrubs. I called for a nurse to get me out of there and when she arrived, she upped the dose of whatever they were giving me in my I.V. I faced the big clock for a flash of a second and faded out before I could throw up again.

Over-calcification in my ear had caused a minor hearing loss (otosclorosis). Surgery missed the mark and left me without equilibrium. The second surgery one week later, failed to correct the error of the first, and in fact left me more dizzy and hospitalized for a longer period. During the following few weeks I felt abandoned by my doctor who couldn't explain my dizziness. He said to give it more time. Friends had a hard time facing me and my husband became my full-time caretaker—feeding me, moving me, washing me, wiping me.

I worked at standing on my own, then walking using a walker. I walked with my husband to a raspberry patch just two blocks from my house. I stood close enough to a raspberry bush to bend over and pluck a juicy morsel into my mouth. I pictured myself doing it, but couldn't manage it. I reached out with my free hand, holding tightly to my walker with the other. I needed only to stretch a matter of inches but could not do it. I thought to myself, "I wish I could pick that berry. I hope I'll be able to go berry-picking again soon." In the meantime, my husband picked raspberries for me.

After a month, I lost the hearing in my treated ear. My doctor still couldn't tell me what was happening. I must have made a hundred calls to specialists who couldn't satisfy my need to understand what was happening to my body and why I wasn't recovering. With time, I moved on to a four-legged cane, and eventually to a regular cane.

The twist in the story begins here. I had the surgery because I wanted to get pregnant and, according to my doctor, pregnancy could make my hearing worse. If I didn't have this routine surgery now, and I got pregnant, I could miss my chance of saving my hearing. Lesson #1: Always get a second opinion.

Thanks to precise technology, I did get pregnant... two weeks after the second surgery. Not a time to recall. I had morning, noon and evening sickness every day of my pregnancy except one and I loved being pregnant so much it didn't matter to me. I hadn't yet been diagnosed as permanently disabled, and I believed I would recover.

My elation about being pregnant overcame my every negative thought. My joy in being pregnant at the ripe age of 43 ignited everything near me, and I threw up with a smile... over and over and over and over. I fell down on the stairs, I fell down in the supermarket, I fell down in a list of locations.

I had a third surgery in Los Angeles, seven months later without general anesthesia. The doctor suspected that my perilymph sac (where your balance juice is stored) had been punctured in the first surgery, and the liquid ran out onto my hearing nerve and killed it. I would be deaf in one ear forever. The surgeon encountered an extraordinary amount of scar tissue, but could not determine its cause. He tried to clear the scar tissue so my perilymph fluid could find its way back into its sac. The doctor said there had been too much damage to clear a pathway. The surgery could not improve my condition and I could expect to be permanently deaf and balance impaired for the rest of my life.

I still didn't believe it. I researched balance disorders, spoke to specialists, practiced walking, brushing my teeth, showering and a thousand daily activities I couldn't accomplish without losing my balance. On the rare occasion that I spoke to my original surgeon, he pleaded with me to undergo a treatment that would kill my equilibrium in my affected ear, and said this would destroy all the false messages my system was receiving. I'd read that this procedure could also make my balance worse.

In one last pregnant vomit, my water broke and shortly after, Alex Oberstein Knudtson was born, four weeks early. 4 lbs., 13 oz. The greatest day of my life. Moments before my C-section, I lost my vision, my blood pressure went sky-high, and the baby's life was in danger. My heart wanted to stop in the middle of surgery. Alex couldn't get out fast enough. Because his lungs were not supposed to have been fully developed, we expected to Medi-Vac him and a neonatal team to Anchorage, 225 miles away. Yet he came out crying and remained in our tiny hospital with me and his jubilant father.

Within weeks, I walked with a cane in one hand and my baby in my other arm. My husband and friends helped me get around. I practiced and practiced and my first doctor told me I wasn't getting better, I was merely learning to compensate. He still wanted to kill the nerve to my equilibrium.

I refused. My Los Angeles doctor said I was as good as I was going to get, but I didn't believe him. I wanted to play with my child. I wanted my life back, to dance again, kayak, ski.

I went to physical therapists but the exercises made me sick. Two years after my original surgery, after three separate individuals recommended I contact HANDLE, I called our local HANDLE representative. I struggled through a frustrating evaluation and began my HANDLE program.

My faithfulness with HANDLE faltered at times. I gave up entirely at times. Nine ear specialists said my balance problem was permanent, unless I killed the nerve, and I still wasn't willing to risk the consequences of another elective surgery.

I continued with HANDLE. I exercised and lost the weight I'd gained from pregnancy and two years of lack of movement. At some point, I occasionally left my walking cane at home, until I didn't use it at all. After less than two years of Face Tapping, Hug and Tug, crazy straws, and more, I learned to ride a bike again, kayak, and play with my son.

Postscript: Sally Oberstein is permanently deaf in one ear and has recovered about 75% of her equilibrium. She still performs her HANDLE program with hopes to recover the remainder of her vestibular functioning.

FROM SCHIZOPHRENIA TO
TRAUMATIC BRAIN INJURY
A POEM BY RUTH KIRSCHNER

I lost hope.

Crying every morning. I called my Mom. I said I did not want to die.

I was forcibly taken to the hospital and locked up, accused of saying that I wanted to kill myself. I have never said that, not to this day.

Help. Someone who'd listen to me deeply is all I wanted. Someone who cared enough to listen deeply to the pain I felt and tried to express.

But that was too difficult for them to understand, so they locked me up, depriving me of that which kept me alive—religious practices and studies.

They tried to get me to take drugs, but I steadfastly refused. Knowing that they had me there for wrong reasons. They forced me to sign a voluntary commitment agreement, giving me false and misleading information about my "rights."

Repeating the same questions over and over again, they interrupted me, and thus avoided hearing my real feelings and pain. Trying to explain what happened and why, their response was that I was psychotic and very, very sick.

Ignoring my feelings. Ignoring my words that were telling them that they were increasing my anxiety. They accused me, "You're here because you said you wanted to kill yourself." I explained to them that I was traumatized by hospitalization following a traumatic brain injury.

"Had I attended special education classes or been held back?" they asked. Oh, how they flattered this 53-year-old woman by suggesting that I went to school so recently! I should have thanked them for it! They knew not that special education wasn't in existence when I went to school. The teachers would not keep back a quiet, obedient, conscientious pupil like me—never. I managed to slide through the system unnoticed. I never caused trouble, so why should teachers be any more intelligent than MDs?

My childhood, my teen years especially, I began paying the price for medical ignorance, despite my mother's tears and pleas for help. The doctors diagnosed me as schizophrenic because I was shy and angry.

Not until after my forced psychiatric hospitalization was I in real danger of dying through suicide. I cried out for help. It came when my mother contacted The HANDLE Institute.

From the first appointment, I felt encouragement and hope; for the first time, no one labeled me or said I was "sick." With a sigh of relief and joy, I changed rapidly.

My youngest sister said I was softer.

My mother said I seemed surer of myself, not always asking her to repeat what she said. Enjoying life, coming alive, according to my mother.

I would not be alive now if it was not for HANDLE.

I have a long way to go.

But now I know I can do it.

Postscript: Ruth Kirschner is a full-time student of Early Childhood Education and Psychology at Boston College.

GOING TO MONTANA
JAN CASE KOERWITZ

My Mom was 78 years young. She was still skillfully driving her '68 Dodge Dart, which she kept in mint condition. She kept the home I grew up in with fresh flowers on the table, raked bags of leaves from the front yard, and was the sunshine in all her friends' and family's lives.

In October of 1998 she was found at the bottom of the basement stairs, unconscious. She suffered a traumatic brain injury and was in a coma for eight days. She spent a month in a foremost brain injury recovery center, where they tried to teach her to talk, eat, dress and walk again. Her hearing turned on one day, amplified, and she was terrified at every sound... and there were plenty of them, 24 hours a day, in this hospital atmosphere. She became sleep deprived and disoriented. It had been a blessing that she was not able to hear during her early recovery and hospital stay. The body is wise. They wanted to use drugs, and all she wanted was some peace and quiet.

The doctors discharged her to my care when she did not meet their criteria for improvement. I took her to her home, to the quiet, restful and aesthetic environment she had created. Her sense of balance would come and go, but she was not cognizant that she had this problem. She would get up and try to walk, crashing to the ground with no warning. I attempted to stay within arm's reach 24 hours a day. Much of those three months are a blur to me now. Her language was still very compromised. I made the commitment to be her caregiver because I knew her so well, and felt I was the only one able to anticipate her needs that she most often could not express. She could feed herself, and enjoyed meals, but she needed help dressing, toileting, bathing and assistance with walking. Her sleep patterns were all over the place. She loved to go for rides in her beloved little yellow car.

Several months after her accident, we had an appointment at The HANDLE Institute to meet with Pamela, the practitioner who had worked the longest with Judith. Mom had been complaining of pain that I thought might be sciatica, as she was spending so much time sitting. I had iced her lower back, but clearly, she was hurting. We had anticipated our meeting with such hope, that we decided to keep the appointment. During her interview, Pamela realized that Mom's pain was too severe to allow her to focus on anything else. Mom was indeed very distracted and overwhelmed. Pamela suggested that we get medical attention. By that afternoon Mom was scheduled for surgery for her broken femur and a partial hip replacement.

A month later Mom was back home, learning to walk again, still with compromised balance, huge challenges with language, and still needing intensive 24 hour attention. She was fussy and bored, and very frustrated. I decided to bring her back to The HANDLE Institute, this time to see Judith. As Judith conducted the session with my mom, I sat quietly in the corner of the room. Mom began to answer Judith's questions in a manner I recognized as her irrational expression (some might call it demented) that characterized her speech so often these days. Mom told Judith about the apple that was growing on one leg, with ivy growing on the tree, and about the egg in the other leg—an egg with a railroad going over it. As I began to tell Mom to refocus, Judith stopped me and told me she was speaking in metaphor, describing the healthy leg and hip and the normal flow of sensation and blood flow, comparing it to the leg with the metal implants and the cold and fragile sense it gave her. I was in awe.

Then Judith began to interview Mom about events in her childhood, trying to get a sense of who this woman was prior to aging and brain injury. Mom again began to speak about things that were unreal—about intense heat building in her, and other descriptions that Judith again told me were metaphors. As Judith finished listening to Mom's descriptions, she turned to me and asked, "Did your mother have rheumatic fever as a girl?" And I gasped. She had. She had just related metaphorically to Judith the entire story of her illness, how it progressed and left her now with hands that caused her great pain because they were too arthritic to allow her to enjoy the activities that had once filled her life.

Mom then, ever diplomatic, had had enough. She was tired. She let Judith know this tactfully, telling her she had to go to Montana. Judith graciously acknowledged that we all had a lot to do that afternoon, and that Montana certainly was a long ways off, so we had best end our session now, so Mom would not be late. She arranged to come out to Mom's home to follow up on our first meeting.

When Judith arrived, Mom wanted nothing to do with her, so Judith and I carried on conversation. Judith showed me the gentle exercises we could do to encourage Mom's healing, re-pathing those signals that were not connecting. It was so clear that Mom knew what she wanted to say, but often the words came out in a jumble, or as opposites, or similars. She asked for a "windowpane of lake." After my work with Judith, I was able to interpret the "window pane" as "glass" and the "lake" as "water." She wanted a glass of water! Now I was starting to understand the complexity of how we learn language, and how our brains access this stored information. I was even surer that I was the one who needed to be there. I know those associations, how she always thought of children as flowers, and when she referred to "the rock" it was the huge rock across the street from her house, and that meant "home."

Judith taught us gentle exercises to stimulate the vestibular system, and because Mom was so resistant to "therapy," Judith helped me think of ways to use every day activities to accomplish the movements necessary. Into our daily routine, we incorporated activities designed to cross the midline, like putting on socks with legs crossed over and moving her right hand over to the left side of her body to polish her fingernails. We took walks around Greenlake, and I pushed her in a wheelchair, gently crossing the midline in the path. We used a crazy straw and played with a pipe to blow a little ball into the air. I learned to watch for the signals that said "too much activity" or not enough stimulation. Her healing brain needed just the right amount. I incorporated Judith's detox recipe into her diet, and did the reflexology regime after her bath. Judith explained that even if I did the exercises in her view, she would benefit from the process of mental rehearsal. So I did.

Because she loved to be in the car, my husband and I loaded her up in our VW Camper and took a "road trip" (all you flower children of the 60's will appreciate this!) We camped along the way, and she thoroughly enjoyed the trip. When we started out, I would sit with her in the back seat, with her supported by a stack of pillows on one side and me on the other, as she could not negotiate to stay sitting up as the car moved and turned. By the third day she was able to maintain her own balance as we drove! Soon she was riding shotgun with my husband, and reading signs aloud along the road.

When our trip began, she could transfer from her seat into her wheelchair, and then we'd ramp her out. By the end of the trip, she was climbing in and out of the van, and rarely used the wheel chair. She still could not walk independently, but we had progress! After five weeks in the VW, we returned home and decided to buy a motor home and continue traveling with her. It seemed to be just the right amount of stimulation, and created many new situations. Judith had taught me the concepts of gently enhancing movements, and with this, we could adapt activities to encourage her healing.

We set out again in the motor home, and about three weeks into the trip, while visiting my in-laws, she experienced the sensation of losing her balance, and responded by trying to catch herself. This was a first! The signals were starting to connect!

Simultaneously she became more and more able to ask for what she needed and to speak out if she was uncomfortable or unhappy. Though her language was still often scrambled, there was a period of clarity each day. She was starting to gain skills that would enable her to be independent, and work with other caregivers.

She was unwilling to do "therapy" so it was by the grace of Judith's non-invasive work that she progressed to a level of safety. Judith's phenomenal ability to understand what Mom was experiencing, and her ability to understand her language, which was a mystery to me much of the time, all contributed to what otherwise was a frightening, helpless, hopeless situation. HANDLE is an approach that can help the countless number of people who face challenges that are not being met in the current medical model. Judith's creative approach to each challenge, based on a keen understanding of how the brain actually functions (not just theory), combined with her personal dedication to helping others, qualify her for sainthood.[1]

---

[1] My personal goal is certainly not sainthood. Rather it is to train innumerable other practitioners how to look at the obvious and do what makes sense. And there's the trick, since it was not obvious to anyone other than myself that Jan's mother was speaking in metaphor. But then, that's one of the glories of sharing these triumphs. Now others, like Jan herself, may perceive things they had not seen before. And it should become obvious that Gentle Enhancement® is the key to working with people who are vulnerable and whose nervous systems are delicate and even damaged. Judith Bluestone

THE GREATEST GIFT
MARSHA KORPI

A t the request of Cathy Stingley, Certified HANDLE Practitioner, Marsha Korpi made the following presentation to a group of HANDLE Interns in her hometown of Homer, Alaska:

Early the morning of June 30, 2001, I found my partner, Tom Keffer, in our yard, with severe trauma to his head. I did not know what had happened to him. The ambulance took him to the hospital and we were taken by Medi-Vac to Anchorage. Tom had a subdural hematoma and required surgery to remove blood clots from between his skull and brain.

For the next month, I traveled back and forth between Anchorage and Homer, working during the week and staying with Tom during the weekends. Although he was expected to recover, Tom remained in a coma and experienced some seizures. His only response was to pin his arms to his sides when the nurses removed his dressing gown.

Tom and Cathy Stingley had been long-time friends. She had, through a mutual friend, let me know that if I would like to call her, she was willing to share some ideas with me that might help Tom. On the third of August, Cathy and I finally got together. I was planning to travel to Anchorage to be with Tom that Friday evening or the next morning. Cathy and I visited awhile and she talked about the HANDLE approach and Gentle Enhancement. She showed me how to do Hug and Tug on fingers and toes and how to do Face Tapping. I tried them and couldn't always get my fingers to alternate on the Face Tapping!

On Saturday morning, Tom's son, Gordon, and I returned to Anchorage. I told Tom about Cathy and started playing with his fingers and toes and then did the Face Tapping. The first time, he fought the Face Tapping, throwing his head around and just not seeming to want it. I said, "Relax, I'm going to do it anyway!"

I had encouraged friends and family to visit Tom and stimulate him, hoping he would come around. Nothing changed. So between Hug and Tug on his toes and fingers and Face Tapping, Gordon and I would talk to him. By the third time, Tom just lay there, not fighting it, and then pushed his face out towards me! Later in the evening, he seemed somewhat aware. The fourth time, he started to open his eyes and look at us. He still seemed a little bit blank, but was looking at us. So we stayed with him into the evening.

Sunday morning we got back to the hospital and another friend, Lady Jane, was there. She had been doing some Reiki, a method of natural healing based on the application of Universal Life Force Energy, with Tom. The first time I did the Face Tapping that morning, he kind of opened his eyes and was stretching his face toward me, as if to say, "Yeah."

The second time I asked, "Tom, do you want me to do your face again?" He nodded yes. Oh, wow, he's communicating! It got to where I could now ask him questions. He couldn't talk because he had a tracheal tube, but he could shake his head, nod his head or shrug his shoulders. That was the first time I had been able to communicate with him in five weeks!

Now that he was communicating, there was a chance to shed some light on what had happened to Tom. My thought when I found him was that a mother moose had kicked him because we had a cow and calf in the yard the night before I found him. I asked him if this is what had happened to him and he shook his head, no.

The real story remains a mystery, but three weeks after his surgery, when the staples were removed, an MRI revealed a series of mini-strokes. It is unknown whether these happened before the head injury or since the head injury. My conclusion is that he probably had a stroke dur-

Tom, a few years before his injury.

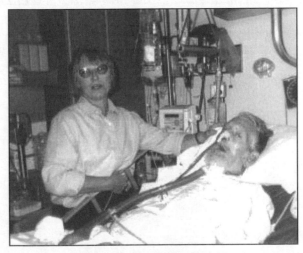

Marsha and Tom on the
Sunday Tom communicated.

ing the night, got up confused, and for some reason was going out to the car. There is a long, winding boardwalk through the trees. There is one place where he could have fallen and hit his head on a birch tree and another where he could have fallen from the boardwalk a distance of about two feet. We will never know.

What we do know is that in five weeks, that particular Sunday was the only time Tom communicated with anyone. Cathy gave me the greatest gift. (Marsha pauses here as tears trail down her cheeks.) It's a happy tear. It's just hard to talk. I needed to head back to Homer Sunday night, so I would be there for work Monday morning. Tom had the tube in his nose, and as I leaned over him I said, "You know, I would love to give you a kiss. Would it hurt if I move the tube away?" He shook his head, no. So I moved the tube and gave him a kiss. He responded; the same thing. I got two kisses from him! We actually got to say goodbye. Monday he began to have seizures again and slipped back into a coma. I received a call to return to Anchorage, and Tom passed away on Wednesday.

I really appreciate Cathy and her willingness to show me the HANDLE exercises. I received the greatest gift of being able to say goodbye.

Postscript: The medical records show that from the day he was taken by Medi-Vac to Anchorage, to the day he died, Tom was in a coma. However, Marsha, Gordon, Lady Jane, and a nurse all witnessed his communication. His daughter, Tracy, asked one of the doctors why this was not in his record. The doctor indicated that he had heard about it, but had not seen it himself. Therefore, it was not entered into his record.

From Sophisticated Compensations
to Innocent Exposure
A Postscript by Judith Bluestone

The triumphs you have witnessed are each very different, one from the other. Yet one thing is certain: a systems approach to neurodevelopment coupled with Gentle Enhancement therapy assisted each person to achieve a better quality of life. Some of the adults you encountered had performed effectively in society at large—getting through years of school, marrying, raising children, working. But their problems caused them great stress. They needed to work harder to compensate themselves for deficits. They were not efficient. Months or years of stress took their toll. And several of the lives you just entered were abruptly altered by traumatic events.

Frequently when adults experience trauma to their bodies and their brains, the physicians and therapists concentrate on determining and dealing with disabilities caused by the specific damage. When they do not apply a systems approach for the person in the current situation and also do not look back over the individual's lifetime to learn what systems were weak and which were strong from earlier stages of development, they frequently overlook the fact that cause and effect may not be closely related in time. Problems that an individual may have had in a particular system, such as weakness in the proprioceptive sense of body in space and/or hypersensitivity to touch, might cause a

49

lack of basic security, a vulnerability. But a bright person, like Ruth, might intuitively compensate for this by applying visual vigilance to assure herself that she was in fact secure. This would make it difficult for her to pay attention and learn in a classroom. And in later life, if her visual functions were suddenly impaired, as they frequently are in closed head injuries, she might experience seemingly psychotic reactions, since she could no longer protect herself in the area of her earlier and basic vulnerability—bodily security in the environment.

As we move into the stories that families share about their precious children, these problems will become more vivid. Young children are not sophisticated enough to camouflage their deficits. If we only take the time to see what their behaviors are telling us, rather than trying to control the behaviors or mask the symptoms, we can truly help. But to do that we must understand a little more about basic neurodevelopment, so when things go awry we know how to intervene.

There are a few systems whose importance becomes evident as you continue to step into the lives of the heroes and heroines in *The Churkendoose Anthology.* You will be hearing about them repeatedly, in different ways.

One of the systems you have already encountered is the vestibular system. Sally's story elucidates many things about this system—that it is part of the inner ear, and that it regulates balance, and more than balance, the general sense of body in space or proprioception. It also regulates muscle tone—the degree of tension in the resting muscle, so each and every part of the body is ready to respond to the motor plans devised by the brain. It is also responsible for how our eyes move to track. And, of course, the ear helps us hear, and this again helps us know our relative position in space, through the ability to echolocate—an ability Sally has lost.

So the inner ear helps us hear, see, balance, know where we are in space, and be ready to respond to any situation. No wonder you will continue to hear that HANDLE programs incorporate vestibular activities. Many other therapies incorporate vestibular activities, but not in the same fashion that HANDLE does. Ours are slow and controlled, without the use of equipment, usually beginning on the floor and isolating the three different axes of the vestibular system, so that each can gain strength without stressing the others—Gentle Enhancement.

Although most of the people we help have vestibular activities included in their programs, the structure of the activities varies from person to person. One may need to do the activities with visual focus, another with eyes closed. One may need to perform only one repetition of the activity initially, or only a fraction of a repetition. Another may need to begin with a dozen repetitions, until the brain stops thinking about the action and just allows it to happen. At that moment, the person who could do 12 slow and controlled back rolls without feeling dizzy because she was working so hard to control the movement may suddenly say, "Whoa!" And from that moment on, she will begin to strengthen the weak system without cognitive processing taking over for functions that should be automatic. Then the whole system—the person—begins to become efficient, and therefore to experience less stress.

You will find the names of certain HANDLE activities mentioned a number of times. Some of these activities are explained in Appendix A. There you will find ones that have few variations and a small number of precautions about implementation. I would not be professionally responsible to share as "over-the-counter" advice, activities that require a great deal of training and individualization for safe and effective enhancement of function. While activities undertaken as isolated events, and not part of an integrated program, rarely yield significant and lasting results, those incorporated in the appendix have helped many people resolve important aspects of their challenges, even without a complete program.

Now, as you continue to enter the lives of families who have turned to HANDLE for help, you will hear many renditions of how a HANDLE practitioner developed a neurodevelopmental profile and guided the individualized program of a child. Some of the descriptions are not technically accurate, but they are the expressions of the families themselves, and so I have allowed them to stand. In doing this, I pay tribute to the power that families have. Without professional knowledge and technical terminology, they still grasp the essence of the matter and implement with love and commitment those procedures that help heal the neurodevelopmental disorders of their children. HANDLE places the empowerment of families to implement guided home-based programs far above demands for using professional jargon correctly. No one can work collaboratively with those she intimidates or embarrasses. And so, I give you the stories of the children, in the words of those who lived them...

PART 3

I'M JUST DIF-FER-ENT

—Ben Ross Berenberg
The Churkendoose
Part Chicken, Turkey, Duck and Goose

What if?
MELISSA GRIFFEN

"Everything before HANDLE is a passing dream. I was in sixth grade when I did the HANDLE program and from the beginning I started to feel and see changes immediately. I started to compare my life before this and I realized that this was only the beginning of the changes. I also realized that I was going to have an easier time at school. As I progressed in my program through The HANDLE Institute my life in general started to become easier, not only my school life, but Life also."

These are Leah's words as she attempted to write how HANDLE affected her life. The fact that Leah could sit down and write this story, by choice, and coherently is a testimony to her work with HANDLE. Six months ago, this wouldn't have happened. She could not have written down the thoughts she was thinking, on her own and when I was not home. She would have dictated them to me and only after a great deal of frustration and fear. It would have taken hours rather than minutes. It would have been at my urging, not her choice. In fact, she would not have consented at all to the submission of this story—she was too vulnerable. And now... the magic unfolds daily.

When I look back at Leah's life with the knowledge that I have learned through our HANDLE experience, I am awed by the strength and perseverance of this child. Her ability to achieve as much success in life as she did is remarkable.

Her father and I knew life was difficult for her. We knew she could not fall asleep easily, that math was hard for her, that learning to read had been a struggle. We knew that Leah did not relate to many other children and found herself often the victim in social situations. We knew that she could erupt angrily or complain endlessly. We knew that she couldn't wear her socks with the seams in, or the tags on her clothes without feeling as if she would wriggle out of her skin. We knew that to Leah the world was a glass half empty; she would list the negatives before finding the positives in life. We knew that she was terribly frightened of many things and that she seemed often to be on the defensive, even when it was not necessary. But she was progressing in school. She was neither at the top nor the bottom of her class. She could read, although she often missed content. With lots of one-on-one attention, she would pick up some concepts in math. She was an avid horseback rider. She had a big heart full of loving and caring for others and spoke with a wisdom beyond her years.

What we did not know was that every day was painful to Leah—physically and emotionally painful in a way that we never imagined. An accidental touch of a piece of paper on her hand or a brush of another student's hand on hers caused intense physical sensations that often resulted in pain. Even our caresses could be painful if they were too tender. And yet, she smiled, she tried, she learned, she lived a relatively functional and happy life. I continue to be at once crushed by the realization that I did not understand how difficult my baby's life was, and inspired by her tenacity, ability to overcome challenges, her spirit.

I remember once when Leah was about two and a half, I was sitting with her on the stairs in our house attempting to get her ready to leave for a fun outing. We had been there for half an hour and we were both in tears. Around us were about 20 pairs of socks and stockings, all discarded because they tickled and she could not wear them. "We have to go," I grunted in pure frustration. "I can't wear them mommy. I am sorry," she wailed. And then we discovered the miracle of turning a sock inside out so the seam doesn't tickle! Ah, the ability to just get dressed and go somewhere!

We always knew that Leah was very bright. Very early, she demonstrated incredible deduction skills. Her birthday is late in the year, so we knew she would be young in her class. We are firm believers in allowing children to play and grow as much as possible in their earlier years. We do not believe in pushing academics. With this in mind, we chose a school that would give Leah the opportunity to do two years of kindergarten. At the end of her first year, it was very clear to all of us that she was not ready to start the academic rigors of first grade. She had a difficult time holding onto her pencil and disliked writing and she showed no interest in learning her alphabet or doing anything other than play. After a second year of kindergarten, she entered first grade. When her spelling was poor, math a foreign language to her, and reading a slow and arduous process, we were told not to push her, she would get it.

We were perplexed. Leah's pencil grip had not improved and she hated to write, even minimally, so her creativity remained bottled up inside of her. And, she began to be victimized by other children. They were little problems, but they started cropping up. The teacher was very impressed by her problem solving skills and didn't think much of it— just kids learning how to get along. I am so grateful that this teacher saw only the good in Leah. It was a saving grace to her self-esteem. Still we could see the increased levels of stress in her and it concerned us. She was increasingly irritable and cranky at home and had an even harder time sleeping than she had before. Clearly, something was causing this child to have to try so hard that it was impinging on her joy in life.

Then second grade. She began to get further behind in reading, and tutoring was recommended. Math was a fight. Hours of tears and yelling—hers and, unfortunately, mine as well. Frustration and failure. She loved science, but that was her only joy at school. She had a few friends but did not feel that she fit in. Unfortunately, her second grade teacher chose to treat Leah's inability to do math with disdain and ridicule in front of the class. When Leah couldn't do the work, instead of helping her, her teacher gave her more work to do. Leah's self esteem plummeted and her progress with it. Her little sister, Kit, would cry when Leah had math homework. She knew what was coming. We needed to find another school and some help for Leah.

About this time we discovered a chiropractic technique called NOT—Neuro-Organizational Technique. She was assessed with some language processing difficulties and we did several months of treatments. This work coupled with a wonderful tutor allowed her to learn to read. We thought we were on the road to relieving Leah of the struggles she was clearly confronting. What I did not realize at the time was that the discomfort that she experienced during the chiropractic treatments was far greater than I understood. This discomfort, of course, undermined the effectiveness of the work and we stopped.

Leah started at a Waldorf school in third grade with a teacher who was sent to us as a gift. (In Waldorf schools the teacher stays with the class through eighth grade.) She provided Leah with time to heal, loving and gentle instruction, and a place to get back on her feet. Leah found her heart again and received encouragement.

Over the next three years, we saw some improvement in her academics. I spent summers with Leah teaching her math. We went back to the basics and by sixth grade she understood, somewhat, what a number was. She could add, subtract and do some multiplication and simple division.

Most of what was said in her lessons passed her by, she could not finish her work, writing was difficult and painful, and she was hiding (we later found out) the fact that she understood very little of the languages she was being taught. She was in a sort of "productive-non-productive" middle ground. She did well enough that she wasn't considered a high-need child, but she was clearly not learning easily. Teachers gave her glowing reports, encouraging us by saying, "She will get it soon. It is clear that she is very smart and tries hard." They commented on what a loving and delightful person she is. It was so ironic—she was having such a hard time, school was so stressful, and yet she seemed so functional—that "she would get it any minute."

Trying hard was not enough. She needed help. But what help? We worked closely with our homeopath and Leah did some special movement therapy designed to open up the energy systems in the body. These helped, but not enough. Having been a teacher myself, I did not want to go the traditional route of having her assessed and finding a band-aid for her. I did not need a label for her. I needed her to be helped from the inside out in a way that would honor her and build on her strengths. I began investigating and we prayed.

During a fortuitous discussion while on a kindergarten hike with Kit's class, I discovered HANDLE. Much gratitude goes to the parent who excitedly shared her child's HANDLE experience with me. Leah's father and I knew instinctively that HANDLE was what we had been searching for and made an appointment to see Judith even before we attended an information evening. After that evening talk, we were even more convinced that HANDLE was the missing piece of the puzzle that could bring Leah's life together. The three months until our appointment seemed an eternity, but it finally arrived amidst hopeful anticipation on our part and hopeful trepidation on Leah's part.

Leah was unsure about HANDLE. She was willing to try it because her father and I told her we really felt it could be the key to making learning so much easier for her. "What if," we said, "just what if learning didn't have to be a struggle? What if this could help you to be able to do all the things that seem to elude you now, all those things that you almost get but are just beyond your grasp? What if?" She consented to try it with all sorts of negotiations for stopping if she didn't like it. Leah took to Judith quickly, felt empowered by Judith's respect, information and encouragement, liked that the activities were fun and therefore diligently did her program.

Leah is blessed with the most amazing teacher (thank you, thank you, thank you!) She is loving and kind and has been so open to accommodate Leah's school program to help facilitate her progress. Most of those accommodations are no longer necessary, but this wonderful woman's insight, perception and loving guidance allowed Leah to gain maximum benefit from her HANDLE program. Between the two of us, we spoke to each one of Leah's teachers and gained their support. As a result, Leah was allowed to relax. Gentle Enhancement was a huge key in Leah's progress. As she was ready to do more, she did. We all honored her perceptions of her own needs, and rather than push her onward, we encouraged her to take breaks and omit what felt too stressful. This seemingly minor thing, allowed Leah to come off the defensive and as a result, she progressed at an amazing rate. (This has been one of my greatest lessons. A little done calmly goes much further than a lot attempted under stress.)

As Leah says, right from the beginning we started to see changes. Suddenly she was able to do things she could not do before. Two months into her HANDLE program, she had made so much progress we all had to remind ourselves that we weren't even halfway through and there was so much more to come!

Six months later, I watch my child beginning to live her life fully. Math sheets are completed in a short period of time; explanations are grasped easily. She's catching balls now that her eyes don't jump around. Therefore, she is much more involved with the games at school. Her handwriting is clearer; she doesn't go over and over the letters, pushing so hard that her fingers become calloused. She finishes her work calmly and on time. She's improved in all her subjects from German to Handwork. And, she is enjoying herself.

Her teacher tells me that Leah is now present and available in class. She raises her hand, offers answers and works readily in groups. Other parents have commented on her industriousness. "Something is different about Leah. What is it?" Daily, she comes home with a "guess what I did today that I couldn't do before" story. "The teacher explained a complicated task orally and I did it. I was the first one done! All my work in my book is complete! I didn't need to have the assignment shortened. I did it all and had time to spare! I copied the work off the board (instead of from a paper next to her) and still finished on time!" Kit sits spellbound as Leah fluently reads to her, book after book. Leah's violin teacher is amazed at how a child, whose sight-reading was laborious at best, is playing difficult pieces brilliantly the first time she sees them. All of these were impossibilities six months ago.

And then there are the more subtle changes. She is much less afraid of the dark. She has a much greater sense of where she is and doesn't get disoriented or scared so easily. She is calmer, so much less stressed. She is participating in conversations now in a different way, because she understands what is being said and follows what is going on. She is softer, calmer, more helpful, and happier at home, making family life easier and more fun for us all.

Along the way we have hit some stumbling blocks. She would regress, and then burst forward with new changes too numerous to remember. The greatest obstacle we encountered was Leah's self-image. She had built a life around being okay with herself as a person who could not do many things, a person who needed to be on alert all the time, a person who was slow and scared and couldn't understand things, and definitely a person who could not do math. As different aspects of her brain and being awoke, these beliefs and her reality no longer matched and Leah didn't know who she was anymore. She was frightened to be capable, to see herself as capable, because it felt like it wasn't her. Judith suggested a practice called EFT— Emotional Freedom Technique. It is a simple and remarkable technique that dislodges blocks in the energy system of the body through a simple sequence of gentle tapping, just as acupuncture might dislodge blocks in the physical body, except no needles! I learned the technique and my remarkable daughter allowed me to work with her to unearth these beliefs and dissolve them. She has released so much pain. She has brought herself to a place where she is building new beliefs about herself, joyously awaiting the next new discovery about herself. I continue to be awed by her strength and depth of spirit and feel honored to be her mother. To see her feel so good about herself is the most amazing gift!

With rapid progress, Leah is catching up with herself. She is learning things that were mysteries for her in 2nd, 3rd, 4th and 5th grade. Academically, interpersonally and in her relationship with herself, Leah is learning and maturing at a remarkable pace. It takes patience, but now she knows she can. Now she knows life doesn't have to be a struggle so much of the time. This new and adventurous world is opening up before her and she is welcoming it.

HANDLE has been a family adventure. The house was filled at times with laughter as Leah and her dad played blow soccer. Kit and Leah would do Hula Hands together amidst squeals of delight as they "got it." Leah and I shared many of the activities. As time went on Leah has become more and more independent with her activities. We have all grown in this process, learning a lot about ourselves as well as about Leah. The journey goes on as Leah's systems continue to integrate the changes and she finds herself stronger, more balanced, growing up with an ever increasing capacity to learn and accomplish what she sets out to do.

The challenge in telling this story is that there is so much to say and yet the words do not seem to do justice to the frustration, pain, joy and blessings of the experience. All parents think their child is extraordinary, and we are no exception. We have always had times with Leah when things went smoothly and she seemed at ease. She was not a "problem child," but a child who, in general, found the world a difficult place to be. There are so many subtleties and things that parents know or perceive about their child. So many ways that Leah's dad and I felt helpless to help her relax and be herself. To watch our child grow from struggling in the world and in herself to embracing the world and gently enjoying her place in it, is a magical experience. At this point, I am clear that we were right; Leah is an extraordinary person, and now she is free to joyfully be all that she can be.

Postscript: Recently, I was speaking on the phone with one of many people that call me to ask about HANDLE. The person asked if Leah felt she received benefit from the program. I asked Leah, who had just entered the room. She beamed and said, "Oh yes! Life is not as frustrating, not as frightening, not as scary (as it was). It's like I am just beginning life now! I'm just waking up! I'm opening to life now!" With tears in my eyes, I reflected that this miracle has come from a crazy straw, a hula hoop, and some silly little games!

"FRED, ARE YOU IN THERE?"
JANE ADAMS

For Bob, life had always been a little bit difficult. He spent the better part of the first two weeks of his life hospitalized. Severe jaundice, due to a blood incompatibility with me, required him to be in an incubator much of the time. We held him as much as we could, but I've always felt that if he could have been attached to me for those first two weeks, he would have been so much more at ease.

Being the first grandchild on both sides, he was adored by many. He had a wonderful personality and showed signs of being very bright. In fact, he seemed to be "very" many things: very cautious, very physically active, very physically sensitive to touches and textures, very apt to be over stimulated in certain situations. I remember a time, at a loud and crowded state fair, when Bob managed to find a quiet pond where he could sit for a few minutes and be calm.

I work as a parent educator, so I have a great deal of information and education about development and children. As parents, we strive to provide an open, loving home for our children, to understand them as individuals and create a home environment in which we can all thrive.

Over the years, we did many things to help make life a little easier for Bob. We recognized his need for quiet time, and for time to process. We understood about the clothes that bothered him, the noises that upset him, the environments that helped him and those that did not. We understood he did not like fast rides or roller coasters. Really, he did not like doing anything too fast. He took his time and got used to things before becoming involved. We went to a naturopath to test for food allergies, and significantly modified his diet.

All of these things helped, but still, life was more challenging for him than for most other children. He had trouble getting to sleep, staying asleep, focusing at school, and with certain noises, textures and temperature changes. When he was little, we had a game we played with his socks. The threads inside bothered him, and the word "thread" sounded like "Fred" when he said it. I would take each sock, open it up and say in a loud voice, "Fred, are you in there? You better get out, because Bob is going to put you on now!" It helped our attitudes, but the sock threads were still a source of irritation. I must have cut every tag out of every shirt and sweatshirt he owned from the time he could tell me they bothered him.

When he reached school age, we sought out a public school program that we thought would give Bob the best opportunity for success. We were extremely fortunate in the teachers he had in those early years. On the first day of first grade, I was very nervous about how he would react to a room full of kids and expectations. His teacher, a veteran educator and wonderful woman, having recognized his temperament right away, sent him outside to sketch the trees during free time. Needless to say, he did well in her class.

His school employed a child-directed learning approach in a multi-age classroom setting, where children are encouraged to manage their own time and many projects. I have often wondered how he might have done in a traditional classroom, having to sit for large portions of the day and learn primarily through listening.

After many years of us tweaking this and that, and helping him learn how to express his needs and feelings, Bob said to me one day that he was actually a little bit afraid almost all of the time. Something about that statement resonated in me, and I realized there was some big piece we hadn't addressed. I had been to a workshop on attachment, and the presenter had mentioned sensory integration and The HANDLE Institute. I got the book, *The Out-of-Sync Child*, and I couldn't put it down. I called HANDLE. After talking with a person there, I discussed the whole thing with my husband, and we made an appointment for Bob. He was just weeks shy of his 11th birthday.

At that time, Bob was having a rough time staying focused and finishing his work. He was struggling to meet the expectation of self-management that was emphasized at his school, and he was not working up to his potential. We'd had several teacher-parent, and even teacher-parent-student conferences, and we were all frustrated. It seemed he knew what to do, but just couldn't do it.

But, Bob didn't want to go to his HANDLE evaluation. He felt that there was something wrong with him, and he'd be labeled dumb or have to go to a special class. In fact, our experience was so positive and validating that Bob left feeling smart, good about himself and very motivated to do the exercises. We were impressed with our whole experience: the respect we received from our practitioner, the professionalism of the staff, the thoroughness of the program. The day of his evaluation, we went out to lunch with some family members between the testing and program set up. Bob was more talkative than usual and quite upbeat. And then we went home with all the resources we needed to begin our program!

We diligently stuck to it and immediately began to see a change—a calmer, more confident Bob—one who no longer had to use all his mental brightness to tough out each day. Because we were integrating his senses, Bob now had energy available to focus, and have fun. His upbeat mood stayed with him from the moment we left HANDLE. The interference had been taken away.

Prior to HANDLE, Bob's mood or behavior would frustrate us both. On most days, we would reach a point where we would get stuck, and not know how to return from this frustrating situation. And then, we found this stopped happening altogether. He learned when he needed to change his thinking or make a different choice, instead of simply complaining that he was miserable.

His teacher commented that it was "eerie in a good way" that Bob could focus and choose to do his work amid even significant distractions. During free choice time one day, Bob was finishing a math assignment so he didn't have to bring it home. That may not seem unusual, except that during this time he was surrounded by three or four boys who were talking to him while he was working. Bob was able to stay focused and finished the assignment while interacting casually with his friends. Over the months that followed, at various family gatherings, family members also commented on the changes in Bob, noticing his calmer and more confident manner. I felt like we were seeing the child who'd been in there all along finally shine.

Bob has made the transition to middle school incredibly well. He manages having several teachers, much more homework, a locker, new friends—all with a positive attitude. The school he attends emphasizes effort, and students are selected for the honor roll based on the effort they put forth, rather than for their letter grades. While he has done fine with his grades, we are most proud that he made the "effort honor roll" the first quarter he attended the school.

And during a recent vacation, Bob couldn't get in enough roller coaster rides! The first day at the theme park we were visiting, he and his brother rode four roller coaster rides in the first hour we were there. We even rode one that "pulled more 'g's' than the space shuttle!"

Bob is now much calmer, happier and more confident. He sleeps better and longer. He tries new foods more readily—even vegetables! Still, he remains cautious with new experiences, but no longer feels afraid most of the time. For this, we are so grateful to have found HANDLE.

UNCOMFORTABLE IN HIS OWN SKIN
ISABELA MADISON

O ur son, Will, is a very special and wonderful six-year-old boy. He has a very vast and deep imagination, is extremely honest, intelligent, sensitive and athletic. He has a strong sense of justice and is quite competitive. Like most parents, we focus on the positive aspects of our child.

As Will grew, we continued to recognize wonderful qualities about our son. At the same time, we began to notice aspects of his temperament that made his life difficult and often made him sad. Of course, this made my husband and me sad too, as well as frustrated and filled with rationalizations and self-doubt. Had we chosen to have Will diagnosed, it is likely that he would have been labeled with ADD, ADHD, Oppositional Defiance Disorder and maybe even a few other acronyms.

Our lives had become increasingly more difficult following the first years of Will's life. Social situations were extremely stressful. He had trouble with impulse control, usually adopting a fight or flight mentality. He never chose to work things out, and never capitulated to anyone.

Punishment seemed to have no effect on Will. Taking away favorite toys or privileges for bad behavior never worked. No tears, no begging or pleading for another chance. He'd even personally bring the toy down for confiscation. You'd think he'd been trained by the CIA.

Will was extremely self-conscious and he disliked feeling

crowded or being watched. He was sensitive in all ways. Clothing had to be just so. Socks couldn't have even the smallest wrinkle before putting on a shoe. Bright lights and loud sounds bothered him. Some of his earliest words were "sun eyes!" He didn't like to be hugged or caressed. Water splashing on his face was intolerable. He insisted on having his face and hands cleaned after eating or if dirty from play. Strangely, though, he liked spicy foods and took a drop of Tabasco sauce on his tongue without a flinch.

Transitions were always a struggle. I learned to give Will prior notice for any change, such as getting ready to leave, to eat, to turn off the TV or if we were expecting a visitor. Everything had to be on Will's terms. In fact, nearly every situation was difficult unless it went as he imagined it.

Our friends with children also lamented the difficulties of child rearing... the tantrums over a pair of shoes or a treat, trouble going to bed or leaving a birthday party. Since Will was our only child at the time, we didn't realize that his intensity was extreme, until our second child, Henry, was born.

Retrospectively, Will's infancy was very difficult. He was not snuggly, nor was he a calm baby. At birth, with eyes wide-open, he seemed to be very aware of his new world. Although he slept miraculously well and long, he spent his waking hours wiggling and pushing while I held him. It was as though he expended so much energy during his waking hours that he would pass out at nap and bed times. He slept through the night immediately, and awoke in the middle of the night only five times that I can remember. He nursed very slowly. Sometimes it would take him 45 minutes to finish eating. He also tended to spike very high fevers.

As a toddler, Will was shy. He avoided social situations, preferring to play with one child at a time in his own home. At 19 months, Will's difficult behavior seemed to balloon. His conduct in organized play situations, such as classes or playgroups, was chaotic. When his nanny took him to these events, he would run like a lunatic, without regard for the other children or parents. His eyes would glaze over, as though he was in another world. At circle time, he would either sit in the middle of the circle, or choose not to participate at all. He was uncomfortable with finger play songs and with any sort of music at all. He was unable to execute simple instructions unless they were repeated numerous times. Even then, he needed to be led physically to the activity. Tantrums were the norm. Later, we learned that other parents asked to be moved to other sessions because he was so wild.

Bedtime became unbearable, and Will had perpetual dark circles under his eyes. He simply would not go to sleep until he passed out. We tried staying with him until he fell asleep, but this could go on until midnight with him playing, begging for another story, jumping and carrying on. We tried letting him fall asleep without us. We tried implementing a rigid schedule. We tried letting him pick the venue and routine... nothing worked. Our pediatrician suggested we get strict and gate him into his room. It took two gates stacked one atop the other. He clung to the gates until he finally fell asleep on the floor, like a dog at the front door. Many days ended with Will screaming in his room and with us on the couch agonizing over his torment.

Play dates at home were becoming increasingly difficult. Will would first hide from his playmate, or would wear a mask, as though he wasn't comfortable in his own skin. It seemed that he wanted to be someone else. He didn't want anyone to look at him. It struck me as paradoxical that he was so extremely self-conscious, yet so unaware of his own body.

He did not want anyone within his "space," and it was his impulse to push others away. This gave him the appearance of being an aggressive child, when in fact he was a very gentle boy who loved to hold babies and softly pet animals.

He was very controlling in his play with other children. If the play didn't go his way, he would abruptly end the activity. He spoke loudly, and liked to play physically using exaggerated body movements. His favorite activity was jumping from high places onto a pile of pillows, arms flailing wildly. Needless to say, we had few repeat play dates.

Will's third birthday was particularly memorable. We invited 10 children to a kid's play center. During the free play, he ran from activity to activity without really playing with anyone. When the time came to do the 'birthday thing' in the party room, Will became very indignant and angry. He didn't want to do the usual things in the usual order. He couldn't bring himself to be happy that his friends were there to celebrate with him. Instead, he was angry with anyone who spoke to him. Pizza and cake were pushed away. He complained about the noise level, the usual laughing and giggling of three-year-old partygoers, and covered his ears. I often reflect on the photo taken of him at the head of the table with his king's crown on his head, a sunken expression on his face and his three-year-old body poised for conflict. It was so sad to see what should have been a fun and exciting event become such a torturous experience for Will, for his guests and for us.

We never dared to send him to other parties without one of us staying for the duration. He wanted the crown, wanted the first piece of cake, wanted to open the presents, never participated in the games, and so on.

When alone with our family my son was relatively more focused and calm. He loved to play with Legos, organize objects in rows and categorize them. He was an early walker and talker and was very athletic and coordinated. He learned to ride a bike with training wheels at three, and gave up the trainers at four and a half. He had a fantastic memory for places and things. At four, he learned to play chess and enjoyed chess camp that summer. It was so frustrating for us, because we recognized his intellect and abilities as "normal," yet he was so different in social and public situations.

Will would rarely tolerate caressing, snuggling or even having his hand held. We thought he was just independent. The bedtime routine, getting dressed, food selection, pushing the crosswalk button, the color of his drinking cup... his whole world had to go according to Will. If things didn't go how he had imagined, he would "melt down." Friends consoled me that all kids do this, and with a renewed sense of security, albeit false, we'd continue on for another few months. Inevitably, we would always come back to the fact that the other kids simply could not be this difficult, with this intensity and for such long durations. One of Will's "melt-downs" could ruin the whole day for us all.

Will's Dad and I would joke that if I said "black," Will would say "white," and vice versa. He was so oppositional that if I offered him his favorite treat, he'd reject it, and ask for a different one. He was so used to controlling every situation that he lost the ability to see that occasionally a suggestion by his Dad or me might actually be something he wanted. For a while, this actually worked to my advantage... until he caught on to my feeble attempt at reverse psychology. The constant struggle between Will and us, and Will and the world, made him angry and temperamental.

Of course, we blamed external forces for his behavior: ourselves, the nanny, the preschool teacher, permissive grandparents. You name it. I was working and couldn't spend enough time with him. The nanny, in our view, was too permissive and couldn't control him. And so on.

When Will was nearing four, Henry was born. I sensed a very different child in Henry, as early as the first days in the hospital. He was calm, nursed quickly, was snuggly and happy. Will loved his little brother. He held him, kissed him. He even helped me change his diaper. I dreamed that somehow Will could absorb some of Henry's calm and affection. For his little brother, I saw true compassion in Will.

One afternoon when Henry was crying in his crib, we heard Will over the monitor saying, "Don't worry, Henry. It's OK. We love you." Another time Will completely broke down with tears when I took Henry upstairs for a "time-out." (Actually, I intended to use this as an opportunity to show Will that he's not the only one who gets punished.) Will was filled with empathy for Henry. "Ah," we thought, "so punishment does affect him. Hmmm, maybe all he needed was a little brother to eliminate the 'only-child' syndrome." More rationalization. Even so, this was a very rejuvenating time for all of us.

As Henry grew older, he had the "normal" tantrums and issues, but the intensity and duration were fractional compared to Will's. When asked to perform a specific task, Henry often did it, and later even responded with "alright." Wow, what a difference. This is when we knew we had to do something about Will. My husband would tell you he knew all along. I thought he was paranoid. He said I was in denial.

We sent Will to preschool, changed nannies and started reading books on difficult, strong willed, spirited children. We went to classes and seminars. All provided some relief, but were focused on changing OUR behavior to defuse the situations, rather than on Will's internal struggle. The classes seemed almost comical. We listened to the parents in the classes describing their child's behavior and thought to ourselves, "These kids are amateurs compared to Will."

Preschool was as crazed as the classes he attended when he was a toddler. He would run around like a lunatic with that glazed look in his eye. He was disruptive during story time and lunch. The teacher felt she couldn't relate to him. I feared the lack of a connection would cause her to dislike my child. Parent–teacher meetings focused on all he did wrong. When I asked what he does well, she looked completely unprepared for this question and had no ready examples. I know what she was thinking: Ritalin. This was heartbreaking, frustrating and angering. However, upon her recommendation, we had him observed by a child psychologist. She was a wonderful woman who gave us ideas on how to change our behavior to help him. Still, we knew he was struggling inside.

The new nanny was very organized, disciplined, consistent and strict. Initially, this seemed to improve his behavior. "Aha," we thought, "maybe just a bit of discipline and structure is all he needed." It didn't take long, though, for Will to look sad when she arrived. He was not having fun and clung to me when she was around. Her stay was short-lived. My husband and I knew that I could not return to work and must stay home with the boys. We knew that we couldn't lay blame anywhere anymore, even though it was only in our own private rationalizations. Still, I didn't know exactly what we could do. For us, drugs were not an option.

My being home calmed Will a bit. He seemed to be happier and somewhat more at ease. But he was still extremely oppositional, controlling and sensitive to hugs and touch. Although he was potty trained during the day, he could not stay dry at night. He was grinding his teeth, and could not fall asleep in the dark. Even though he usually slept at least 12 hours a night, he had perpetual dark circles under his eyes. None of these things seemed to alarm our pediatrician, who assured us that he would outgrow it.

As he approached five, Will started a two-year kindergarten program. We selected a developmentally focused, child-oriented school. We hoped that the school's holistic approach to learning and life would help us help Will to succeed on his own terms.

Will really enjoyed the structure and routine of kindergarten, liked his teacher and his classmates. But it was very difficult to get him dressed, fed and out the door in time for school. The pants had to be the right ones, with the elastic in the back. Shorts in the winter, long pants in the summer. The shirt had to be un-tucked. He wanted to select breakfast, but refused to tell me what he wanted.

This, of course, was a time when I needed him to do what I asked so he would get to school on time. So it was also a time for him to do exactly the opposite of what he knew I wanted from him. We spent many mornings with me screaming and with him crying. I felt terribly guilty and angry at the same time.

At school, he seemed to be playing with the boys who were similar to him. Although he was the imitator, instead of the instigator, he was always getting into trouble for being wild, not following directions and being generally disruptive to the rest of the class during story, snack and circle time. It was as though he just didn't know what to do to fit in. He followed only the worst examples.

His immaturity was becoming more obvious to us. Neighborhood kids of the same age seemed to be one to two years more advanced socially than Will. We could see that Will sensed it too. He was most comfortable playing with younger children, very flexible children and with other kids who displayed similar behaviors.

Late fall, in Will's first year of Kindergarten, his school hosted a seminar for parents entitled, "Beyond Labels." The seminar was presented by The HANDLE Institute. It was described as a discussion on how to help children with difficult behaviors, without drugs. This really hit home with us. We had long been searching for a solution that focused on the cause of the behavior rather than on treating the symptoms. Immediately afterward, I scheduled Will for his first session with the HANDLE therapist. This was in early January when Will was a bit over five years old.

At the first session, Will was in his glory. He kindly displayed all of his usual behaviors without much prompting. The therapist was able to see his full repertoire. Her extremely calm, caring and interested demeanor endeared her to Will. He willingly performed the tasks she needed to see to complete her evaluation. And she uncovered additional problems that we had not noticed, such as his inability to grasp a pencil with three fingers, something a five year old should be able to do.

We left with 13 specific activities to do daily until our next session. The activities included various exercises, games and massages. The therapist also provided us with several additional suggestions, including dietary changes, a review of possible allergens and a suggestion for a listening program. I was a bit skeptical, but hopeful.

We worked on the activities nearly every day for three weeks. To my complete joy, and some surprise, we started to notice that Will was calmer, slightly less controlling and had fewer problems controlling his impulses. He had a few *really* good days at school, according to his teacher. He managed to be very sweet while at a friend's house, while the same friend was quite unkind. Unprompted, our baby-sitter mentioned that she noticed that his behavior had improved. To be honest, I still did not disregard the possibility that this behavioral change was due simply to the additional attention he was getting from Mom and Dad during this time.

Our second visit with the HANDLE practitioner, three weeks later, refined a few exercises that Will disliked or had mastered, and added a few new ones. Will spoke so fondly of the therapist and he seemed to enjoy our visits, looking forward to the next one. We had no trouble doing our exercises and massages dutifully. He was excited to return to learn more ways to help him "learn how to act," as he put it. He sensed that these activities were helping him. We were amazed because he didn't resist.

Within the next two months, our home life became more calm. Will was controlling his temper and was increasingly happier and more comfortable with himself. His play with friends was becoming more cooperative. An overnight ski trip with a friend, who typically knows how to "push his buttons," was without incident. They laughed and played. His teeth grinding decreased. He even learned to use chopsticks, albeit awkwardly. He was becoming more affectionate, which is something I had assumed would never happen. He was letting me hug him and caress his head. This still brings tears to my eyes. I became a believer in the HANDLE method. We continued the exercises for three to four more months.

At school, his behavior was improving. With tears in her eyes, Will's teacher told me that she was able to make a connection with Will. The wild activities had decreased and he seemed calmer. However, he still had difficulty following directions at school. His self-control had improved somewhat, but it was not yet automatic.

Two months later, we met with our therapist for the last

time. The purpose was to discuss the fact that Will's behavior was improving significantly at home, but the pace of improvement at school was slower. Will's current teacher was leaving and we were concerned that a new, rookie teacher may not be as patient. The new teacher certainly would not be able to compare the year over year progress. He would know only the conditions at the time.

Our therapist explained that Will was trying to make the social strides that his body did not allow him to make before. He was learning to socialize and interact with the world. His peers had had three years to do what he was trying to accomplish in the one year... but he was catching up! We had to be patient.

Upon our therapist's recommendation, we purchased and implemented the Tomatis Listening Program. This program aims to address Will's auditory processing issues and improve his ability to execute directions. His brain had difficulty prioritizing sounds. For example, he would hear the lawn mower next door to be as important as instruction from his teacher. Imagine what a classroom full of kids did to him.

After completing the eight-week program at home, Will became interested in music. He recognized classical pieces from the Tomatis Listening Program, started to enjoy listening to children's songs, was participating in circle time at school and argued with me as to which music radio station we should listen... loudly.

At Will's urging and pleading, he began group piano lessons three months ago. He was able to sit patiently, listen to instruction and execute each new lesson. He was even able to play simple pieces with two hands within the first three months of class. He became able to focus on long stories, and we finished the four Harry Potter books in less than three months.

It has been exactly one year since our first visit with HANDLE. In general, life has improved markedly for the family. However, we still have work to do. Will's ability to process and execute directions needs improvement. Although he is sleeping 12 hours at night, his dark circles have not disappeared. His impulse control has greatly improved, but he is still behind his peers in this area.

Our plan now is to focus on the dietary recommendations made by our therapist, research how foods affect his behavior, and pin down and address Will's allergies through natural methods instead of drugs.

Will has spent three months with the new kindergarten teacher. As expected, the new teacher has trouble understanding the change in Will from the prior school year. Sure, Will's not a perfectly docile and obedient student. This would be unrealistic. But, he now helps to set the table for snack, greets other children by name, responds when an adult addresses him, asks if he can join a game and brags when he is the first to appear when the teacher calls the class to his side. The new teacher recognizes Will's strengths and has no concerns about sending him on to first grade next year. Parent-teacher conferences are now a very pleasant and productive exchange of ideas.

He is getting along with most kids now. I no longer have anxiety about birthday parties or social situations. His behavior is well within the acceptable realm. Strangers in the grocery store have even accused Will of being a very well mannered young man. This is BIG.

At home now, Will is frequently known to say, "Okay, let's do it your way." Miraculous!

Reckless and Out of Control
Hannah Jameson

Unlike his older sister, my son, Charlie, was hyperactive even in utero. As a baby, he slept very little. "Blessed" with an abundance of energy, he walked early and was on the go from morning until night.

Without question, he was a handful. Anyone caring for him could expect jumps from high places, sudden disappearances and a tendency to "bounce off the walls." When being read to, he could sit for a long time, but would then absolutely explode with pent-up energy. Often, Charlie was a whirlwind when everyone else was exhausted, and we would send him to run round and round the house to keep from severely punishing him. I struggled to keep up with him and wondered if he would "grow out of it."

Up to this point, we were a home-school family and Charlie did not have to contend with a school setting, where he most likely would have been unmanageable, labeled ADD and had his self-esteem damaged. Charlie, however, had a sweet, outgoing temperament and made friends everywhere he went.

But, when he did enter school at age twelve, he was often in trouble for fidgeting and being unable to sit and concentrate. His teachers acknowledged his intelligence and creativity, but keeping him going on structured schoolwork was quite challenging. Working with Charlie on homework assignments, and trying to keep him on track, was as much work as repeating the grade in school myself!

About this time, Charlie's behavior at home began to deteriorate. Meals had always been a difficult time, but now they took on the quality of a nightmare, with him fidgeting incessantly, jumping up from the table and running in and out of the room. This went on until someone lost patience and yelled at him, or forced him to eat in solitude.

Charlie was reckless and out of control. There were times when he needed to be physically restrained, and times when we considered calling the police. Consequences for poor behavior included long periods alone in his room, removal of privileges, possessions or money. And I am ashamed to admit that hands were raised in anger more than once.

We sought the help of a counselor. She told us that she saw no evidence of ADD, and that we simply needed to learn how to negotiate and relate better. Following her advice set us back on finding help for him for months.

I had read many books about ADD, hoping to find something to help my son. In my work as a healthcare professional, and especially in my work with children with disabilities, I developed a strong skepticism regarding the use of labels, such as ADD, and the use of medication as a quick fix.

All the same, I knew my son needed help. There were a number of individuals in my family, including my father, two brothers and three nephews, who had been diagnosed with attention problems. My older brother, who my son most resembled in behavior, led a life that was a disaster in every way: three divorces, financial bankruptcy, a series of unfulfilling jobs, a number of troubled children. My intelligent and creative father was never able to work a day in his life, and spent his last years living in a van without a friend in the world. It became a nightmare to watch my once sweet, sparkly, puckish, creative child head down a road that could only mean the end of so many hopes and dreams for him.

I feel incredibly lucky to have stumbled onto a mention of The HANDLE Institute, and to have been able to take an introductory workshop from Judith Bluestone. Following the workshop, I typed up my notes, enlarged them, and posted them on the wall of my office, hoping to understand more of the most insightful and practical approach to helping my son that I had seen.

A few months after his thirteenth birthday, Charlie had his HANDLE assessment that was conducted by Judy Russell in a most thoughtful, careful and respectful way. Charlie's system was so sensitive that on the first day of his program he was able to do his vestibular exercises only once each, vomited and was sick the rest of the day. Although Judy carefully explained his program to him, and his chores at home were cut back so he could do HANDLE daily, Charlie was not always cooperative. We saw few results in the first months, and it required discipline to continue.

Yet, after about three months, I began to notice a decrease in the number of "meltdowns" he had, and he appeared to be growing a bit more thoughtful about his behavior. When he was tired, his behavior would revert, but as time went on, he became more in control of himself. He calmed down, and his ceaseless movement and random behavior lessoned. He became more pleasant. School became easier.

For eight months, with a two-week break after six months, Charlie continued with a HANDLE program, altered periodically to meet changing needs. Today, his behavior and his ability to concentrate are so much improved that he is like a different person. He has less difficulty falling asleep. He gets along better with his peers and teachers because he shows more restraint, even when he is annoyed or stressed. For several years running, Charlie had had very severe headaches, which we had always connected with dehydration. Each time, he would end up in bed. He also got headaches at school from the light of the overhead projector. Since his HANDLE program, the headaches have diminished and he has had almost none in the last year. I suspect that the HANDLE activities designed to correct his light sensitivity are responsible.

It makes me sad to think that there are so many children suffering from similar neurodevelopmental problems, and instead of getting help, they are labeled as bad children. Charlie still has attention issues, and we are pursuing other non-drug treatments such as neurofeedback, but I will be forever grateful to Judith Bluestone and Judy Russell for helping save him when his life could have been a catastrophe.

HANGING ON FOR THE RIDE
MARIE HURST

All children have their failures and triumphs. But, when a child struggles—with school, with life—the failures are more bitter, the triumphs more sweet. And so it was for Jamie, whose emotions swung like a pendulum between giddiness and despair. And so it was for me, immersed in maternal apprehension and concern for her future. This is the story of Jamie's sweet triumph over adversity, and how she has arrived at the best idea of herself.

Exactly when Jamie's difficulties began is impossible to know. As a baby, Jamie captivated and drew smiles with her bright and delightful ways. An easy baby, her early independence and natural curiosity were evident. By nine months, chubby legs propelled her stiff, but steady, baby walk and she could prattle an impressive number of multisyllabic words. She appeared to be developing beautifully.

Had we been aware, however, had we known what to look for, the signs were there in toddlerhood. Jamie was our first child, and her father and I didn't recognize that her unwillingness to dress herself, inconsistency with toilet training, indifference to her tricycle, books and puzzles and her impressive tantrums were signs of anything more than a strong-willed temperament. "Terrible twos" lingered into three, four and five.

With equal measures of negotiation, circumvention and patience, Jamie and I nimbly danced the dance through the rhythms of our days at home. Her preschool experience, however, was less harmonious as she was not compliant in this structured environment. Problems cropped up intermittently, and it was not uncommon for her to act aggressively toward the other children. As frequently as not, she was disinterested in the activities that tempted her age mates, favoring the pursuit of her own passions. I recall her preschool teacher commenting that, at any given moment, Jamie could be either the happiest or the unhappiest child in the school. Nevertheless, her teachers considered her bright, highly imaginative and academically ready for kindergarten.

"Marching to her own drummer" was the theme of her kindergarten year, and her teacher recommended that she repeat kindergarten to be given extra time to mature socially and emotionally. After much consideration, we consented given that she was, at the time, the youngest in her class. Although her second year of kindergarten progressed more smoothly, the academic demands of first grade set off a downward spiral of poor conduct and poor scholastic achievement for Jamie.

Jamie's first grade days were punctuated with tears, and occasional show-stopping tantrums, as the sights and sounds of the classroom easily overwhelmed her. The rigor of full-day instruction proved especially distressing and she would sometimes tune out and retreat into her own imaginary world. Transitions were the trickiest of times, and her stress was unmistakable as she sat at her desk tearing papers into tiny bits or chewing her hair. On days when I received the dreaded phone call from her teacher detailing yet another impropriety, I alternated between alarm and despair. On days when she came home from school to melt into a sobbing heap on the floor, my heart broke for her.

And if tantrums at school were not enough to isolate her socially, her driving desire to touch things and others sifted her out wholly. Fleeting eye contact made it difficult for her to read social cues, and she could recall scarce few of her classmates' names. Despite a tender heart, a wide-open smile and a wit beyond her years, Jamie established few friendships in these early years.

Without doubt, Jamie was intelligent, but by the end of first grade, she began to fall behind her peers academically. Of chief concern was her handwriting. Gifted with an active imagination, creating stories, poems and songs was both a strength and a source of pleasure. Committing them to paper, however, was excruciatingly slow and physically painful due to an awkward and tense pencil grip. With writing came feelings of failure, so she often flat-out refused to do it. When she did, her writing was hopelessly illegible, wrought with reversals, uneven spacing and poor letter formation. As the rest of the class began incorporating accurate spelling into their writing, Jamie was unable to break away from the phonetic "invented" spelling techniques taught to her in kindergarten.

Helping Jamie learn her assigned spelling words was nothing short of frightening for me. Words rehearsed just moments before would be lost, as if sucked into a black hole. How such a clever and articulate child could remember the details of an outfit worn on her third birthday, words to a song she'd heard just once, or the length of a giraffe's tongue from a classmate's book report, but not a spelling word consisting of four letters, defied all sense.

Jamie's thinking was, in a word, inflexible. She could be "stuck" on certain ideas, seemingly stubborn to those working with her. Once stuck, she had difficulty devising solutions to her problems until she was able to distance herself from them with time.

P.E. class was simply a succession of "owies," and she balked at the competitiveness. Timid in the face of physical activities requiring balance, skill or coordination, seven-year-old Jamie had not yet learned to ride a two-wheel bike or swim. Consequently, she avoided popular childhood games, retreating instead to the safety of solo fantasy play. In this, she missed important opportunities for social learning, and she seemed to prefer lingering in her imagination to the companionship of other children.

Jamie tried to control her environment as a means of reducing her anxiety in the classroom, but her teacher construed her behavior as oppositional. "Busy hands," always on the move during instruction, made her appear as if she was not listening. Although, if anyone took the time to ask her, it was clear that she had absorbed every word.

It's always been that adults have had strong reactions to Jamie, either finding her energy and playfulness objectionable, or delighting in it. Jamie's first grade teacher was just two years into her profession, and Jamie's behavior shook her confidence terribly. A tug-o-war over control developed; the harder Jamie pulled her end, the harder the teacher worked to exert control over Jamie. And, it was not always Jamie who fell in the mud. This did not endear her to her teacher.

I began to dread my time as a volunteer in the classroom. I would ache as I watched Jamie's anxiety build from transition to transition toward the final crescendo of tears. Like a snowball barreling downhill, and I was powerless to stop it. Never have I felt so helpless, as a parent or otherwise. I found myself avoiding her teacher because it was so hard to listen, week over week, about what had gone wrong, about how Jamie differed from her peers. At home, my stomach began to turn flips as 3:00 approached, anticipating what I might hear of the day's happenings. I jumped when the phone rang. My emotions were raw, and it took all my reserves to check the tears that lived just below the surface. I was not always successful. There were many tears that year.

Jamie was a "standout," to be sure, and this was not a compliment. Although her teacher appreciated her exuberance and sense of humor, she described her as a highly distractible and sometimes difficult child. Jamie tried. She worked hard and wanted to succeed. Yet, she inevitably ended up frustrated. That Jamie's school career—her happiness—were in jeopardy, was now clear and undeniable.

And so I set out in search of solutions, intent on finding relief for my young malcontent. I was compelled, in fact, and it is what saved me from drowning under a tidal wave of misery. I read. What I learned about dietary interventions intrigued me, and so I eliminated dairy products and artificial ingredients from her diet, just to see what would happen. Nothing, as I suspected, since she didn't display the classic signs of craving, intolerance or allergy. Nevertheless, it was too simple a thing not to try; she deserved at least that. I persevered.

I talked with others in similar situations. Repeatedly, they advised me to seek counsel from a professional, yet I was resistant to this notion for reasons that I wasn't able to articulate at the time. Defying my intuition, we did finally visit a highly recommended child psychiatrist. Hoping for insight into the motivation behind Jamie's behavior, we instead received recommendations for medication and psychotherapy.

Over the years, I had heard Jamie labeled in many ways: immature, undisciplined, easily frustrated, stubborn... Yet the labels offered up by the professional we saw, I was unwilling to accept. To reduce my inquisitive, compassionate, funny and brave little girl to a set of dysfunctional behaviors was, to me, offensive. I could not take that step out onto the slippery slope of preconception and lowered expectations, particularly since the labels offered nothing by way of insight into Jamie's behavior beyond a description of it. Moreover, I resisted the labels as a means of resisting the prognosis that accompanied the labels: school failure, teenage angst, drug use, jobs lost, relationships failed. To these disheartening predictions, I thumbed my nose, feeling as defiant to authority as my young daughter must have often felt.

I turned my attention to finding ways to give Jamie more control over her environment. I researched various alternatives in education and was prepared to withdraw Jamie from public school in favor of home schooling. Yet still, feeling sure that there must be something better, I continued my quest.

It was a crisp, sunny day in early March when Jamie's teacher called. "Please come and pick her up. She's having a bad day and I cannot teach with her pacing the back of the room." I made a decision this day; it was to be her last day in the public school. How could I put her back into a situation that was clearly causing her anguish? My conscience would not allow it. I brought Jamie home, set her at the kitchen table with her beloved box of art supplies, and I went to work.

I spent the rest of that day making inquiries into some of the therapies that had, over the weeks and months, caught my attention: Developmental Optometry, Auditory Integration Therapy, Neurofeedback. Then I ran across an ad for The HANDLE Institute and picked up the phone. I spoke with someone who patiently, patiently answered my many questions. Huh! Her motion sickness has something to do with this. I knew it! Intuitively, I knew it. I remember thinking that, had this conversation not been about my own child, it would have been fascinating. But, I was not quite ready for that. I hung up the phone and paced the floor, thinking long and hard about what I had heard, while Jamie immersed herself in her creations one floor below. I began to settle into the thought that I just might find the elusive answers for which I had been searching. I sent Jamie back to school the next day.

Then I attended a HANDLE community information presentation and was introduced to ideas brand new to me. I learned how the functioning of the eyes influences behavior, learning and the ability to socialize and attend. I learned that the relationship between the two sides of the brain affects ease of learning and emotional states. Ah, yes! I learned that how one uses her body affects the organization of the brain. I learned about the plasticity of the brain and its amazing capabilities of renewal and reparation. And, in contrast to anything I'd heard before, I learned that The HANDLE Institute was applying these concepts to help children and adults alike overcome neurological deficits.

The essence of compassion and respect embodied in the HANDLE approach drew me in fully. Up to this point, I had encountered, at best, a disregard for Jamie as an individual. Rather than speaking to Jamie, some spoke about her as if she wasn't in the room. I bristled at others' observations that she would be better behaved if only I would be more strict with her. Well, perhaps so, but Jamie evoked in me a desire to nurture and protect, not control through punishments and rewards.

When the principal of Jamie's school wanted to place her on a "behavior plan," I refused. Aside from being demeaning, a smiley-face sticker on a chart was not going to solve this problem. Concealed under Jamie's bravado was a vulnerability that must have been difficult for the school staff to reconcile, because if they had, surely they would have recognized their solution as faulty. My instincts dictated that such a device belied consideration of the problem and would merely add to her misery and amplify her "acting out." From our HANDLE experience, I gleaned an understanding of Jamie's difficulties that lent rationale to my position on this. Discovering The HANDLE Institute felt a bit like coming home.

In Jamie's circumstance, I was also opposed to using the special services of the school. I understood their arguments, yet I felt that singling her out would shine a white-hot spotlight on her weaknesses. I was, and am, certain that no "academic standard" should be allowed to supersede or compromise Jamie's sense of self, for without a positive self-perception of what use is knowledge? As her parents, we knew her best, and we were in the best position to choose her course and oversee her progress. The HANDLE approach allowed us this.

Undoubtedly, the school staff considered me as much of a problem as they did Jamie. Despite my contention with the school, however, optimism began to replace uncertainty. I had found a path that I could tread with confidence and hope, beginning from a position of strength.

At her HANDLE assessment, I learned a good deal more about the impetus behind Jamie's behavior. Many things began to clarify and coalesce in my mind. As such, it did not surprise me to learn that Jamie was unable to shift facilely between the left and right hemispheres of her brain. This helped to explain her abrupt emotional shifts and why she sometimes became "stuck."

An understanding of the vestibular system provided the link between Jamie's poor balance, predisposition to motion sickness and less-than-perfect visual functioning. It was also not surprising to learn that she had difficulty sensing where various parts of her body were in relation to herself, as she sometimes miscalculated her movements and collided with things or people in her path. Tactile and kinesthetic irregularities were impairing her ability to express her thoughts in writing. She had difficulty sensing where her hand was, and what movement it had made, unless she monitored each movement visually. If she paid close attention to her hand, then she became frustrated at losing the ideas she had wanted to capture. Tactile sensitivities also shaped her choices in clothing and she dressed for comfort, rather than fashion as many of her first grade classmates did. Now I understood why socks that left the house on her feet often returned home in her backpack.

That her eyes did not serve her well made perfect sense, as she sometimes lost her place and tired quickly while reading. This clarified for me why some activities could hold her attention beautifully, and why she would invent all manner of distractions to avoid doing others. It depended upon the demands the task made on her already stressed visual system!

Together, these obstacles were preventing Jamie from meeting expectations, principally her own. What a burden my young one had been laboring under! Mingled feelings of sadness and regret, relief and hope, surfaced with the evaluation results. It was no wonder she was frustrated by her difficulty to prove herself despite all the positive qualities she possessed. How could her learning and behavior improve before these root problems were identified and treated?

Eager to have things going better for her, Jamie began her HANDLE program. The downward spiral that began in first grade slowed, then stopped, and then gradually shifted direction. Change washed over her quietly, but unmistakably, like a cool breeze on a summer day. Tears and temper tantrums began to diminish. By the end of first grade, she could read for longer periods and, consequently, her reading skills began to flourish. By summer, the girl who previously cried at the prospect of getting her face wet in the bathtub was jumping off the diving board and had learned to swim. She had mastered her two-wheel bike and managed handily through an 800-mile road trip without a single pit stop for carsickness.

Her Dad and I felt as if the foundation had now been laid for her success in public school. Chiefly, she now needed to fill in the gaps of learning that had eluded her thus far in her academic journey. We were certain that she would need to work hard to catch up, but that it would be, in many ways, an important year for her. We rescinded our decision to home school, and she returned to her public school for second grade. It was what she had wanted to do.

Jamie eagerly anticipated each new day of learning, as many avenues of knowing now lay wide before her. Her first trimester report card held this comment, "I feel Jamie is experiencing one of the biggest growth times of her life and I am just happily hanging on for the ride." Her teacher was right. That many barriers had been brought down was revealed in her behavior. As a regular volunteer in her classroom, I observed a child well integrated into the rhythms and routines of the day. Surely, most parents take this for granted, but, for me, it was a thrill to behold, my first taste of sweet triumph. Early on in the year, Jamie announced, "Second grade is a lot calmer." Clearly, it was she that was calmer. Emerging was a more poised and composed Jamie, as if she had discovered a lower set point for her emotional state. I, too, began to relax.

Remnants of her turbulent start in school have now all but disappeared. If second grade was her year to polish-up her behavior, third grade may prove to be her breakout year both academically and socially. She reads well, and she reads for pleasure. It is with some misgiving that I impound her flashlight at night, long after she should be asleep. She is enthusiastic about math and she seems to show a flair for it.

Assigned spelling words once took her hours to commit to memory, and even then didn't guarantee that she would be able to summon them at test time. They are now absorbed and retained with just a few minutes of practice each day, and she's yet to miss one on a weekly spelling test. She completes her homework independently. These small things, taken together, have added a measure of serenity to our family life.

With better balance, coordination and motor planning Jamie is orchestrating well the movements of her body. She rides horses and participates in gymnastics, activities that would once have been far too demanding and frustrating for her. This winter, we took her to a local ski area for a lesson. As I watched her trudge off through the snow with a group of beginning skiers, I envisioned her, defeated and unhappy, abandoning her ski class for hot chocolate in the lodge. Since my expectancy was unbearable, I found myself at the foot of the "bunny hill" trying to catch a glimpse of her. And, there she was, sitting next to her instructor, floating up into the sky on a chair hanging from a string. Although I'd done it a hundred times myself, the sight surprised me. When I caught her eye, she broke into a huge grin and her thumb flew upward toward the sky. She was having fun! With both hands, I waved wildly, feeling only a little bit foolish, since what I really wanted to do was draw the attention of everyone on the mountain to my child's amazing feat. It was the best day of skiing I had ever had.

Writing has been a promenade of two steps forward and one-step back, but in view is an unmistakable glimmer of a sure and capable writer. A follow-up visit to HANDLE at the end of second grade hastened her progress, and her once undecipherable scrawl has now come under her control— not yet graceful, but fully functional. The samples of Jamie's writing on the following page say it all.

I have yet to feel casual about watching Jamie's pencil glide along her paper, a defining moment, somehow symbolizing the culmination of all that we have been working toward. And I witness, with awe and joy, Jamie's exhilaration with her own progress and a developing love for writing as a means of self-expression. When she grows up, she wants to be a writer—and, oh yeah, a veterinarian, too.

Jamie now has friends, invitations to play, kids with whom to hang at school. As with any child, any person

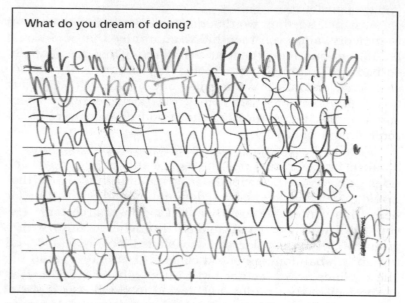

What do you dream of doing?

I dream about Publishing my ghost book series, I love thinking of and fiinding stories. I make new visons and evin a series. I evin make up a name that go with every day life.

A sample of Jamie's writing from the end of second grade.

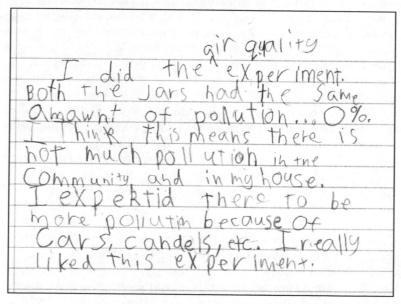

air quality
I did the ^experiment.
Both the jars had the same
amawnt of polution... 0%.
I think this means there is
not much pollution in the
community and in my house.
I expektid there to be
more pollutin because of
cars, candels, etc. I really
liked this experiment.

Jamie's writing less than six months later,
at the beginning of third grade.

really, she has her areas to work: memorizing those thorny multiplication tables has been hard, and applying what she knows about spelling to her writing, well, it's tuff. But she no longer stands out from her peers in negative ways. And without question, Jamie's struggles have bestowed upon her gifts she would otherwise not have known—a keen imagination, developed as a first line of defense, which will be her companion always; a sense of compassion for the underdog; the knowledge of triumph that comes from facing a challenge and emerging victorious.

Judith once told us that we would forget—that memories of our trials with Jamie would dissipate with time. In that moment, I just smiled, sure that the impressions made by her rocky start in school would never fade. Yet, fade they did. To tell this story, I realized that I was having to delve deep to recall the memories, feelings really, of my restlessness and distraction when she was away at school, of the need to tread gingerly and anticipate what might cause her to unglue, of the pervasive unease about what lay ahead for her. In lockstep with Jamie's progress, I have been able to lift my head from this problem and to see beyond it. In doing so, I see that our story begs to be shared. And so it is, through this writing, that I make my small contribution, express my gratitude and offer my words to others as a ray of hope.

WHO WILL PROTECT US FROM OUR OWN VULNERABILITIES?

A POSTSCRIPT BY JUDITH BLUESTONE

From Leah to Jamie, we have seen how, at different ages, problems of sensory-motor disorganization cause frustration. Frustration for parents. Frustration for teachers. And most of all, frustration for the children who look so normal, until they need to respond to certain aspects of their environment. And then, because of irregularities in their nervous systems—central, autonomic and enteric—they cannot respond. Rather they react, frequently reflexively, out of control. They are caught in a trap, trying to perform against odds that are stacked in favor of those other children, their peers, whose sensitivities do not impede their sensibilities. Of course, Will and Bob and the others must protect themselves from their own vulnerabilities, unseen by others. And in doing this, they show us moods that are black, conduct that is destructive, and spirits that are under attack.

Their innocent behaviors, however, do tell us what is wrong, if we only take the time to see what they are saying. From self-isolation to unusual pencil grasp, from poor eye contact to weak math skills, each of these is a window into weak and irregular systems. And each window has a place on the frame of the house that is the neurodevelopmental profile of a life that is developing out of kilter. And the mere fact that these brave children continue to try to meet the demands of each new day is a sign of their desire to achieve, to have us be satisfied with their achievements, to be proud of themselves.

How many times did you read the word "socks" in the stories of these brave children? What is so bothersome about socks, or tags, or top sheets on beds? These wicked little threads and corners poke us in sensitive areas, when we are unaware and trying to concentrate on something else, or simply trying to sleep. The sense of touch is the most primitive sense. It develops in the first month in utero. And at the moment of birth it needs to undergo a tremendous transition, from being practiced in a wet environment through self-stimulation, to being experienced in a dry world, no longer under our control. For those of us who have sensitivities to touch, the world is a threatening place. A pencil moving in our hand can irritate our sensitive fingertips. Food of different textures can annoy our lips and tongues and gums and palates.

And the children who are the most bothered by these sensations outside of their control are children currently classified in the Autism Spectrum Disorder—children who will not allow themselves to be touched, who shed their clothes in public, and yet engage in a lot of touching to fill their basic human need for touch.

Children and adults whose behaviors bring them to be labeled with some disorder within the Autism Spectrum have other sensitivities, too. Not unlike Will, they have hypersensitivity to sound. But their central nervous system sensitivities are so many and their enteric nervous system and immune systems may be so weak, that their autonomic nervous system is continuously stressed, just trying to brace against constant bombardment from a hostile environment. Sometimes, as they protect themselves they close down to activities, and it may be the behaviors that they do not exhibit that provide us the biggest clues into the puzzle of their neurodevelopmental profile. Not the presence of rocking and hand flapping, but the absence of a full range of rocking or the inability to move one hand without the other. Not the biting and swallowing of Styrofoam cups and the gnawing of shirtsleeves, but the lack of chewing food. Not the tantrums over having their nails cut but the blocking of sensations on their faces or the seemingly high tolerance for pain in general. These are some of the many clues we must uncover if we are to help unlock these children from the traps of their own irregular systems.

And while the medical establishment is spending hundreds of months and billions of dollars to discover the cause of autism and a cure for this disorder that has been classified as a disease, parents are quietly and surely moving their children beyond the closed doors of this label, using many of the same activities whose names you are becoming familiar with—Face Tapping, vestibular activities, crazy straws. How these and other HANDLE activities resolve autistic behaviors in children and adults is the subject of another book I am writing. But the stories of the families that follow, and the triumphs of their children, reveal what is possible.

PART 4

I HAVE MORE BRAINS THAN I HAVE LUCK

—Ben Ross Berenberg
The Churkendoose
Part Chicken, Turkey, Duck and Goose

ON A ROLL

LINDA SEVERS

When a friend suggested I check out a non-drug approach to help our son Justin's autism, we were intrigued and optimistic.

Our adventure with autism began in 1995, before we were even aware of autistic spectrum disorders, and the other world of developmental disabilities. Our happy and healthy six-month-old son was hospitalized, shortly after his regular vaccine, when he spiked a fever that wouldn't ease up. After I.V. antibiotics, he recovered quickly and the doctor released him 48 hours later.

But, Justin was not the same child. Over the next 18 months, we came to realize that his delayed speech, inconsolable crying, repetitive behaviors, eczema, irregular bowels and fleeting eye contact were symptoms of autism.

The next few years were typical of most families with an autistic child. There were many doctors, therapists, therapies, diets, drugs, supplements, schools, consultants and hope.

We always believed that we would be one of those success stories you read about in magazines. The fantasy goes something like this: We go for our annual check-up. Jus greets the doctor and has a check-up like a typical child. The doctor freaks, asks how I did it and then rips up the paper with the word "autism" on it. Freed of the label, we return home to a "normal life." I then write that article for the magazine.

We are not quite there yet. Our physicians could only tweak Justin's medications, and our experiments with Justin were getting wilder and less realistic. We were frustrated and discouraged, but not without hope!

Our dream was to find a program to address the cracks in Justin's foundation. Years of speech therapy, occupational therapy and behavior therapy simply didn't go to the root of the problem. Our biological interventions had only taken us so far, and the meds were simply a band-aid. We also realized that we couldn't rely on professionals to do the job for us. Ultimately, we were the ones who would see Jus through for the long haul and live by the decisions we made today. Was this as far as we could take Jus? My gut said no! We wanted our child to grow to be happy, healthy and independent.

Enter HANDLE, our turn to take an active, hands-on role in Justin's future.

Our HANDLE journey started with a trip to Seattle in February 2001. Despite a major snowstorm and power failure, we met up with Pamela Ruffner at The HANDLE Institute office and haven't looked back.

During the intake session, Pamela saw the best and worst of Justin. We shared our concerns regarding Justin's inappropriate behaviors—the high-pitched screams, the aggression, the silly antics, our concerns for his physical safety in the community and his public nudity. We spoke about Justin's self-imposed vegan diet, his preference for loud music, TV and computer simultaneously, and his reluctance to cooperate at school or at home. He insisted on wearing the same T-shirt every day. He had problems with toileting, teeth grinding, self-help skills, fine-motor activities and very limited, purely functional language. Justin's repetition of others' words and phrases was becoming a constant distraction. In addition, his stubborn adherence to his own home-based agenda severely cramped our family life.

We were desperate to understand why these issues were so ingrained and what we could do to break the chain. We were fascinated with the breadth of Pamela's observations and the detail in our prescribed program. Pamela never suggested chemical restraints or anti-depressants as remedies. She considered nothing irrelevant or minor. The whole child—and our whole family—were constant considerations.

Our initial program focused on the very basics. Even after years of sensory integration therapy, Justin's vestibular and proprioceptive systems, the systems that deal with how the body perceives itself in space and how the brain processes the information it gets from the different senses, were immature. We are working on this core element of his nervous system to this day. In addition, Pamela suggested activities to strengthen Justin's binocular vision and muscle tone. With the ultimate goal of ridding ourselves of Zoloft and Ritalin, Pamela showed us a reflexology and massage routine to reduce anxiety.

So far, our results are directly related to how hard we persevere. The times when we slack off, or are unable to complete our HANDLE program, are Justin's worst times. In the beginning, Justin would only watch us perform the activities in front of him. Pamela advised us that "mental rehearsal" was still beneficial. We stuck with it. Slowly, he began to participate in some of the activities and would then let us push him a little in the ones he found challenging. Some he refused outright and still haven't been woven into our repertoire. Other activities have evolved and are now pleasurable things that we enjoy in our quality time together.

My greatest joy has been learning activities we can do together, almost anywhere, that I know are helping him. Some of them are harder and more work than others—we still can't get Jus to suck—but we have managed to keep a relaxed attitude. He has picked up on most of the activities and will occasionally initiate an activity, or just spontaneously do a "burrito roll" himself! One of the greatest surprises has been the desire of our whole family to participate in the program. Justin's two older sisters and their friends have joined in a HANDLE session or two, and have been great videographers at our long-distance program review times.

The best way to describe Justin's results is to say that he is "on a roll." He is completely toilet trained, has had minimal bouts of aggression, is no longer disrobing in public. And dare I say, Justin has not had a high-pitched scream in months. His teeth grinding is only occasional, and he sings in music class. For the first time in over a year, he wore a different T-shirt, and even tried a baseball cap. He is at grade level in reading (grade two), loves computers, bowling, swimming and music.

There are still major issues with family outings, haircuts, conversational language, socializing and self-help skills. But, he is initiating verbally and participating more in our family life. It has been almost a year since we began our HANDLE program and we are determined to take Justin's program as far as we can. Pamela's support and acceptance of Justin as a unique and capable child have meant the world to our family, and to his success. We feel very fortunate to have found HANDLE and to have had the opportunity to work with such a dedicated and experienced team.

THE UNCHARTED TERRITORY OF RAISING IVY
CHARMA JONES

Ivy's first birthday is all a blur to me now. Pictures are the only things that bring back faded memories of that special day. She was smiling, laughing, having fun, dancing to the words of "Happy Birthday." Kisses to all.

So much has transpired since then. As I am sure it is with most parents of autistic children, there has been so much work, so many struggles and so many sleepless, tearful nights. We could write a book on that alone.

And the uncertainty—will she ever talk, walk, read? Will I ever hear her beautiful voice say those beautiful words, "I love you too, Mom?" What will she do when I am gone? Who will take care of my child? I supposed that these questions would never be answered, so I shoved them far back into my mind. Besides, I was already flooded by the day-to-day toils. "Get off of the refrigerator, please. Don't smack your head on the sidewalk. I'm sorry she's screaming. Ivy, you need to wear clothes, we are shopping." All were everyday declarations. And the one most said, "She doesn't talk."

Although it was years ago, I would swear it was just yesterday. It all seems to blur together—the chaos of the numerous appointments and the uncharted territory of just raising Ivy.

This is something about Ivy. And something about how she became the beautiful kindergartner that is now fully functional and seeking out approval from peers. At this very instant, she is looking into my eyes asking, "I want a cookie, please?" She still speaks most of her words in broken English, but she is only six, and she WILL learn. HANDLE is the oil that got all Ivy's gears moving.

Twenty months into Ivy's life, I thought I had gone crazy. "Am I just imagining that she was talking last week? Singing Winnie the Pooh? I'd swear she was playing and smiling just last month at that movie we went to see." Her pediatrician assured me that this was a stage, and that all kids stop talking at some point. Eight months passed and still the pediatrician asserted that the stage would break. He would not listen to my concerns about the sleepless nights, the constant rocking, head banging and screaming bundle of frustration that had become Ivy. I didn't understand how that could have been a stage. That "stage" has lasted for four years.

Ava, Ivy's older sister, had not gone through this. With Ivy, it was impossible for me to enter a shopping center. Ivy would immediately panic. We began walking everywhere because Ivy could not stand the car ride. I could not stand to see her in so much pain.

It was cold season on the west coast of Washington State. Sure enough, with me working in the public schools, I caught a cold and gave it to Ava. We ended up at the pediatrician's office. When we got there, I discovered that our pediatrician was on vacation. "Oh great! Can we please be seen by someone else, then?" They said they would try. I signed in just as Ivy was jumping from the counter to the floor. I picked her up and went to the waiting room.

While we waited, I was thinking, "She never hears me. She has to be deaf." My mother had mentioned it to me a few times and I wondered if she was right.

Soon they called our name. I think Ivy's screams made them hustle a bit. In came a woman pediatrician I had never seen. (To tell you the truth, I cannot find her name on any of Ivy's files. If you are her, thanks a million, you listened.)

Ivy was running around the room and throwing herself into the wall. The pediatrician stared at Ivy. I quickly tried to divert her attention to Ava, who was indeed diagnosed with a cold. "It will pass," the pediatrician said. "Ivy, on the other hand, seems to have a behavior problem. Do you have a communication problem with her?" I explained that

I felt she was deaf, and yes, Attention Deficit Disorder runs in my family and I am dyslexic. She made a quick call and had asked if I could be at an appointment a month later. "Yes, I can." The appointment was with a child psychologist. I felt both unsettled and relieved at the same time. Finally, someone is going to tell me my child is deaf. We will get the needed surgery and it will be all better.

In January of 1998, at the age of two years and eight months, doctors at Mary Bridge Hospital diagnosed Ivy with "severe language deficits." A formal cognitive evaluation could not be completed "given her young age and active, impulsive behavior." Words of the Pediatric Psychologist. This made me ill, as I knew there was something more. And so I went on a learning excursion.

I had been told not be a "renegade parent." I feel strongly that if I hadn't, Ivy would not be where she is today.

My learning took us to the Tacoma Learning Center. Evaluations ensued. The evaluation report contained these words: self injurious, short attention span, self stimulating behaviors, no interest in peers, reduced eye contact. Ivy was 33 months old and she was assessed at a developmental age of 21 to 22 months: social skills, 24-month level; language development, 23-month level; independence, 35 month level; motor skills, 20-month level.

But, they were a great group of people there. They started Ivy in sensory therapy and this was the hardest time for me. Having your child in "the program" meant you met with the therapist (for the big people.) During these sessions, Ivy was in the classroom getting her therapy, and I was so worried because she was without me. The therapist, however, turned out to be the voice of reason. He reminded me that I am a person, even without Ivy stuck to my side, and counseled me to find myself so that I could be a better parent for Ivy. Thank you so much, Joel, for all your help.

In February 1999, we moved to Iowa. Before we left, I threw out Ivy's pacifier and let her watch me. She seemed to be fine, so that was the end of the pacifier. Maybe we were both ready to move on. When we got set up in Iowa, we decided to give potty training a try. We were persistent and it paid off.

In August, we were seen at the University of Iowa Hospital and Clinic. I had heard great things about them being the foremost authority on the study of developmental delays. More evaluations followed and they told me the same thing that I had heard from every other doctor, "She seemed to have a communication and behavior problem, with autistic tendencies."

At this time, Ivy was sleeping only three hours at night, and did not take a nap. When I brought this up to the team, their answer was drugs. My husband and I were very opposed to this. No one seemed to have any answers for us, not even advice on dealing with her blatant disregard for authority.

We looked into numerous therapies and "miracle cures." I was feeling frustrated that she was coming up on school age with no hope that she would ever attend. But, we did receive a letter from the school district stating that she was to attend. I called the district to let them know that this was impossible; a mistake. I laughed and I cried, and they didn't believe me—until they saw her. She soon started her first "special education" class.

We had learned that persistence was the way to teach Ivy. We could get her to eat, use the toilet and say "no." We started trying to get her to write her name, but she always wrote it in mirror image, no matter how insistent we were. Her behavior and actions were still harsh, and we still had no answers for "what was making her do this."

Angie Knowles and Denise Richardson were her special education teachers. They were super. They taught her sign language for potty, so we knew. Teaching Ivy to sign seemed to help her a little with communication. Angie and Denise were always searching for answers to our never-ending questions. One of them mentioned the Early Developmental Intervention unit, where Barb Kaufmann was applying the HANDLE approach to neurodevelopment. Angie had had experience with it with another autistic student. She said we might look into it.

We called and made an appointment. I swear the anticipation almost killed me that week, as it always did when we found a window for our closed box little girl. My husband was worried about my high hopes and had always consoled me after our letdowns. Ava asked if they were going to give her another shot to make her all better. All I could do was hold Ava and listen to her go on about how much she loved her sister even though she bit, hit and tore up her things. Ivy always did have a great support group in her sister, grandparents, parents and friends.

The office had a treadmill in the waiting room. I was immediately aware of it because I recognized it as something from which Ivy would jump. Barb Kaufman came to the door and said, "Come on back. Just let her act like herself." All I could think was, "Great, Ivy will have her hogtied in a second." But, I must have sensed something in Barb that comforted my frustration, aggravation and pain. Ivy must have also because she went to Barb and sat in her lap. It made me cry. Ivy never went to anyone. Barb gave Ivy a pad of paper and she started scribbling. Barb spoke with us—and with Ivy. This was impressive. Until now, I was the only one that spoke *to* Ivy, not about her. Ivy soon finished her picture with her famous mirror image name. I asked Barb why she does that, not expecting an answer. Barb replied with, "Both sides of her brain are working separately and not together." Barb went on to explain how some autistic children can feel threatened by their environment. Their systems are, in essence, jammed. She then explained the vestibular system and how Ivy seemed to be dealing with tactile hypersensitivities, vestibular irregularities, proprioceptive weakness, light sensitivities and probable difficulties with binocularity. WOW! I was in awe, not at the medical terms, but at the fact she had an answer.

I was so relieved. Someone knew what was going on! Then it hit me she might have a solution. She picked Ivy up out of her lap and looked into her eyes. She told Ivy and me that there is a therapy called HANDLE, and if Ivy is ready we will start getting her system undimmed so that it will make her feel a little more comfortable with us. I had been trying to force Ivy into my world, but didn't stop to think that I might need to come into her world to walk her into mine. We made a follow up appointment.

That night, Tim, my husband, and I talked about what Barb had said. We were both relieved at her explanations of why Ivy is the way she is, how HANDLE can work for her and, better yet, why it works. We started that week. Barb gave us some things to do at home like Face Tapping, which proved to be an amazing tool, and joint compression. Goodness, she was able to control her jumping around! And, she was not throwing herself nearly as much. Ivy also noticed her need for these activities, coming to me from time to time grabbing my hands and tapping her face, or giving me her balled up fist so I would squeeze it.

I started to comprehend why certain behaviors happened, and better yet, she started to understand me and what I was asking. Ivy soon had no need for the 3D glasses and special colored highlighter. Her brain was working in the right direction. We knew because she wrote her name in the correct manner all the time.

We soon stepped up into craniosacral therapy. I will never forget the first time Barb had Ivy's head in her hands. After a few minutes, Ivy looked straight into my eyes and said, "Please help me, Mommy." Barb and I both cried. The following sessions were filled with the alphabet verbally, and signing it with both hands simultaneously. Words followed soon.

All aspects of HANDLE have made a difference in Ivy's life. Recently, on a family trip, Ivy stayed in her seatbelt the entire trip to Mississippi. While there, she befriended a gecko that she found. She slept with him that night in her hand. She was so gentle, finally comprehending her own strength. Ivy's list of successes is a long one, if you will bear with me. She is now in full time kindergarten, mainstreamed in public school. Her eye contact is remarkable on down to her eye contact with herself in the mirror as she administers her hairspray and barrettes in the morning. She washes her face, brushes her teeth and dresses herself. She seeks out conversation with peers. I watched her one day walking down the hallway of her school, talking with a boy in front of her. She walks beside me in the grocery store grabbing groceries for me, with not even one scream from her. Her emotions are under control.

The best yet is that we've had a son. At first, we were concerned, due to Ivy's history of violent behavior, about how she might be with him. When we brought him home and she looked at him, "Ohhhhhh baby boy" came from her mouth. Then she sat and held him for the longest time, kissing him and, if you can believe it, she re-changed him after watching me change his diaper.

By the way, every night when I put her to bed at 7:00 p.m. she tells me, "I love you too, Mom." And for that I have to say thank you so very much to Barb for bringing my daughter back to me. It is so nice to listen to her sing Winnie the Pooh once again.

JUST A LATE TALKER
RITA BANNER

Our son is only six, but our journey has seemed much longer. Until he was 18 months old, his development was very typical. He said a few words, pointed to airplanes flying overhead, was very affectionate. A robust and handsome baby, Conner attracted a lot of attention. We had no cause for concern.

When he started daycare for the first time, though, we noticed that he didn't talk as much as other children his age. We brought our concern to his pediatrician who assured us our son was just a late talker, and besides, he was developing typically in all other areas. The pediatrician did suggest, though, that it wouldn't hurt to have his hearing tested. And this marked the beginning.

Since, Conner has had a BAER hearing test, MRI, EKG, allergy screening and a variety of assessments by specialists. Still, none of the experts could explain why he wasn't talking, since everything appeared to be normal about his health and development, except language. He was very coordinated, had a typical attention span, could dress himself with simple clothing and had a food repertoire similar to other children his age.

At about age three, the phrase "autistic spectrum" was introduced. Just as quickly, three different neurologists dismissed it. Then another specialist suggested it again. Ugh! By that point, we didn't care about a diagnosis; we wanted someone to provide us with guidance on helping our son. The best any specialist could do was refer us to a reading list and give us phone numbers to various organizations. There we were, looking for help, and instead we were piled under a mountain of information with no clear direction. It was frustrating and overwhelming.

We decided to look at our local resources, of which there were few because of our rural location. We decided to enroll Conner in a preschool program through our local school district. Conner's teacher was a godsend and we felt, for the first time, that we were doing something beneficial for him. He attended preschool between the ages of three and a half and five and a half. We hired private speech therapists and occupational therapists to come to our house to supplement his program and teach us techniques to use at home. Finally, we felt like we were making progress! Keep in mind, we were referred to none of these resources by the specialists we saw. We conducted all of our own research at home.

Through a connection of our occupational therapist, we learned about Auditory Integration Therapy. It sounded like something we were willing to try with our son. We are not parents who try every program, therapy or diet that comes to our attention. We read, talk and investigate. If it feels right, we try it. If it doesn't, we shelve the information and save it for further reference.

The Auditory Integration Therapy has been useful for our son, and we saw changes in him even before the ther apy ended. He listened better to questions and responded more quickly. He seemed to get more enjoyment out of the music, and began making his own selections. It was during one of his listening sessions that another mother mentioned HANDLE. When I asked Conner's therapist about HANDLE, she was very much in favor of having us try it. The therapist made the call and was able to arrange an appointment for the next day. I was so happy. The positive things I had heard from the other mother made me so hopeful!

Just six months ago, we met Judy Russell, our HANDLE practitioner. She set us up with a daily program of exercises, the majority aimed at strengthening Conner's vestibular system to help him with self-regulation and movement. The exercises are easy and fun and Conner participates willingly. Best of all, we are really seeing results!

Conner's activity level is less erratic and there seems to

be more intent in his actions. Recently, at a meeting with Judy and Conner's speech pathologist, we all noticed that he was able to sit and watch an entire video. This stirred up a little excitement from the adults, as he had not been able to sit for any length of time when we first started his HANDLE program.

Conner began kindergarten this year. He likes school and everyone involved with him has noticed big changes. He is more able to stay on task and he is more cooperative. Catching, kicking and throwing balls is easier now, so Conner is enjoying playground games and is being included in more activities. He was even a line leader in the Christmas pageant!

Our son now falls asleep easier at night, and we have noticed that his rhythm is better. He is able to sit through a haircut and is no longer shaking his hand in front of his face. He has stopped grinding his teeth and he is better able to tolerate teeth brushing.

He is just beginning to develop his speech. We are hearing more sounds that are spontaneous and even a little language. Our recent thrill came when Conner uttered, "Sorry Grandma." Although he has a long way to go with speech, his ability to communicate has improved because his eye contact is better and he is more able to focus and stay with conversations and direction. He listens to questions and is quicker to attempt an answer or an acknowledgement. This encourages people to continue to dialogue with him.

Every child has a different reason why a specific therapy helps him or her. We believe that the HANDLE approach is one of the few that can help any child, regardless of the problems they face. We are so happy to have found it.

GULLIVER'S JOURNEY
SUZANNE FLYNN

He didn't talk. "No problem," they said. "Lots of boys are late talkers. He's still under two. One day he'll pop out with a whole sentence. And besides, all those steroids as an infant probably delayed his development a little." It was obvious he would talk, because he could already read, extremely well.

Everyone was an expert. Everyone and no one. He didn't talk, not until age 26 months and not until we enrolled him in speech therapy. "Developmental verbal dyspraxia," they said. "Let's try for a vocabulary of 100 words by the end of a year." Scary pronouncement but bam: he had 100 words within weeks. Elation. Relief. Either the diagnosis was wrong or he'd staged a miracle recovery. No matter. We were home free; we had a "normal" child. A double relief considering our many trials: earlier surgeries for vascular tumors around his eyeball, followed by steroid-induced growth retardation and vision therapy and eyeglasses.

He wasn't "fixed," though. A few months later, he had not progressed in a linear fashion. His vocabulary grew, but his "communication" skills did not. He still referred to himself as "Gulliver," never "I" or "me." He had no concept of "you" at all. He would stand by the door, looking out and saying, "Gulliver will go outside," over and over, as if the door would open in response to his robotic chant. He would say to a peer, "Austin will give that book to Gulliver," completely befuddling his pint-sized listener.

Most notably, he didn't ask questions. Not even single-word questions, such as "Ball?" or "Cookie?" or "Boo-boo?" There was no rising intonation, no eyebrow lift, no waiting for response.

When he finally did ask an authentic question about three months after his third birthday, it was as if he had lifted off and flown around the room. Once again, though, there was no opening of the floodgates; it was just a "spike" on the graphs, and he was back to his disordered communication. I worked hard to teach him the concept of questions. I made a chart of Where, When, Why, Who and put little pictures next to each word. I trained him to repeat, "Where is the dog?" and "What color is the cat?" and he would sit on my lap pointing and repeating. It felt so futile and rote, and he was three years old. I got him to look at faces by showing him that the eyes and nose form a triangle; because he was so enamored of geometry and shapes, this was a revelation. He wasn't really "looking" at me, but he was looking in the direction of me. It was something. A baby step.

About that time, my sister gave me some information from the Autism Research Institute in California. When I filled out the E-2 questionnaire, my son registered as autistic. The confluence of that "score" and his behavior during that time sent me into a blizzard of despair. I called experts on autism, researched on-line, and arranged for an evaluation through the school district's early intervention program.

We limped along for the next seven or eight months, with no particular direction. Despite speech therapy and occupational therapy, our child continued to distance himself and exhibit a range of difficulties in functional areas. Four-year-old Gulliver was not yet toilet trained. He fought bowel movements with a ferocity of amazing proportion, clenching his gluteal muscles until his face turned purple and his eyes watered. He licked around his mouth and drooled, creating open sores beneath and beside his lips. He echoed phrases. He spun things; coins, checkers, tops, jacks, yo-yos, whatever he could spin. He spent long hours flipping the pages of books and staring at Christmas lights.

Then we found The HANDLE Institute.

The session with Judith Bluestone was a revelation. Unlike other "assessors," she didn't ask Gulliver to perform anything in particular. She sat on the floor and observed him as he explored the toys and games in the room and her interview with us was very thorough. Not confined to the garden-variety developmental areas (walking, talking, toilet training,) the questions spooled through the circumstances of his birth, his eating habits, his idiosyncrasies and preferences, our memories of his infancy.

Judith was respectful and calm. The room was comfortable and welcoming. She made a videotape of the entire session, and the videotape belonged to us, for later reference if we wanted.

And in the end we received no score, no label. What we heard was, "Well, he's really not doing too bad, but he's working a lot harder than he should have to."

Bingo!

We felt exactly the same. We didn't really want to change the essential Gulliver, but we did see that life was more challenging than we'd like it to be.

Ms. Bluestone made many observations of our son. She noted that he favored one side of his body over the other, he was reluctant to look in a particular direction, he resisted closing his eyes and he didn't like things touching the palms of his hands.

We took home a raft of papers detailing exercises and dietary suggestions, and we went to work. The exercises—body movements, face tapping, visual play, blowing, sucking, arm bouncing—were not complicated, and they gave us a sense of purpose. Because we'd done speech and language related therapies for nearly two years, we were old hands at setting up "sessions" with our child. At first things were frustrating. We'd resort to simply demonstrating the exercises, or we'd manage to get only a part of one done. We kept a chart in the kitchen and marked down when and what.

And the improvements filtered in, sometimes dramatically, sometimes in small subtle puffs. I documented them in e-mails to Judith:

This morning we were looking at a book and Gulliver asked, "What's that pig doing?" I said, "He's cutting down that tree with a saw." Gulliver said, "We'll have to fix it." I said, "No, when you cut down a tree, you can't fix it. It's cut down forever." He thought for a moment and then said, looking at me, "Maybe a man will bring a new tree." This is so thrilling. He has never before introduced a new concept like that. As you observed, he is concerned with the here and now, what he can see and touch. But this time he took the trouble to THINK about the situation and offer a solution, or at least a possibility. Never before. I was amazed. He speaks only of the concrete and immediate, he does NOT express ideas. So this was very dramatic. I was thrilled. "That's a great idea!" I said.

We're doing more verbal exchanges, and his creativity is growing. He loves math, so: "What is two plus two?" I ask. And it goes on this way for a while. But then, I decided to change the game a little. "What does Gulliver plus Mommy make?" I asked. "That makes two," he said. He was playing with his ever-present quilt so I asked, "What does quilt plus Mommy make?" And he said, "Two."

"Two WHAT?" I asked.

"Two... (he paused)... things that are quilts and mommies!"

The "old" Gulliver would have left the room or said, "That's too hard, don't tell me that!"

He cried. You know, he never used to cry. Not as an infant when he'd had painful procedures, not later when he split his lip falling on the deck or crushed his finger in the stroller mechanism. He hated crying. But he cried. I asked him, "Why were you crying?" He has trouble, still, with why questions, and he couldn't say. So I prompted, "I was crying because..." and he said, "I was crying because... because... I was crying because I wanted somebody to make me happy."

Last night we blew bubbles together. "I'm skillfuller than you," he said. And he was right! He doesn't want to sleep alone now. He says, "I want to sleep where there's a PERSON," and he comes into our bed. We are thrilled, even though it cuts into our sleep most of the time. He's been doing this for the last month or so, on and off. If he didn't KICK so much...

He is really, really affectionate now, always wanting to be beside one of us, or on a lap. "Stay here with me for a few minutes," he says at bedtime. He also tipped his head ALL THE WAY BACK for hair rinsing last night. That's something he's always been reluctant to do.

Overall he continues to improve, mainly in the area of

language. He is MUCH more contrary and resistant than he used to be, saying "NO!" a lot more often and telling me, "I don't wanna see you, go AWAY!" Yesterday he said, "I'm never ever, ever going to see you again forever." And SHOUTING... such things as "I mean it!" and "Do NOT do that!" and, "I told you NOT to do that!"

I wanted to share something that made me laugh. Gulliver always procrastinates in the morning. He never wants to get ready for school. I always give him lead time, but he still complains. So yesterday, I was in the bathroom and I said, "OK, in 15 minutes you have to get your shoes on. I'm giving you lots of warning." There was silence for a moment and then he said, "I'm giving you lots of whining."

This reminds me of another morning when I told him to hurry up. He said, "I'm not ready, like a fruit that isn't ripe."

His receptive language has really improved. So often he used to not understand things said to him, and now we can talk to him almost as if he were an adult. Best, when he doesn't understand, he says, "What did you ask me?" instead of just clamming up.

Gulliver got angry with me this week and sputtered, "You're not very livable." I asked if he meant "lovable" and he assured me that no, he meant I was unlivable!

He didn't want to go into the store with me, even though we were going to buy carob chips for HIS cookies. I finally asked quietly, "Well, can you at least tell me WHY you don't want to go in?" and he said, "Because there's music in there, and G-sharp isn't happy with C." Can't take him anywhere...

I got a book, The Illustrated Guide to Physics, at the library and he is enchanted by it. Now that he knows the temperature of the center of our sun, I do not hear the end of it!

I worried terribly about his theory of mind, and I tested it when he was about five and a half. He flunked the test. But by just past six he had it. And he was becoming more of a "human" all the time. Another email:

A sort of breakthrough tonight; Gulliver did something really bad—threw a very hard ball directly at my face, to which I turned just in time to have it hit me in the ear, and boy did it hurt. I was very harsh with him. I railed quite a bit about it and told him he had to stay in his room, and that I didn't want to talk to him until he came out. "When someone talks, you have to ANSWER," he bellowed. And he kept pleading through the door and saying it was MY fault, that I started it (because I had done something he didn't want me to do, something completely benign and irrelevant), that it wasn't fair for him to have to stay in his room. I really spoke very sternly to him about how serious it is when you hurt another person and that it's OK to get very mad but that you can't hit someone. "You should have gotten out of the way!" he said.

In any case, it was a transforming experience of sorts, because he began crying. And he cried more than I have heard him cry in his entire life, and I let him cry in there, even though he kept yelling for me to come in. He said it was my job to love him no matter what he did, that's what parents are for. Anyway, to make a long story a lot less long, we had a rather remarkable conversation about consideration and tolerance. And he told me that even though he knows he's supposed to apologize, he doesn't like to do it. I said, "I know, but it's important nevertheless." Then he said, "It's so amazing, you know what? When I cry a lot, I do start to feel sorry." And then he said, "You have to keep talking to me because if you don't we won't be in love any more!" He hugged me for a very long time and I cried too and told him I didn't like to feel so angry but that I was very scared seeing that ball come at my face... and we sat hugging for a long time, just talking... and it was the best language I have heard from him ever, then and afterward. Maybe I should get into a fracas with him every week, eh???

Despite the improvements and our happiness with HANDLE's programs, we still had challenges. He was "thrown out" of Montessori school because of his inability to stay on task, complete assignments and not irritate the other children. He had trouble understanding "personal space" and the loudness of his voice. But HANDLE didn't abandon us; we got new exercises. And his awareness grew. Reading with a book "wrapped around" his face helped him hear the loudness of his voice. A balance board helped him feel more comfortable with his position in reference to others. He learned how to "guess," to anticipate, and to be a little more flexible. His memory expanded. His handwriting improved.

In the supermarket today, I couldn't believe it. A clerk asked Gulliver six or seven questions, and he answered every single one with perfect eye contact and no trepidation. This has never happened. I am beside myself. And so proud. So, so proud.

And last night at the supermarket, we were in the produce section and he said to a nearby clerk, "Hi!" Big smile, eye contact. I was flabbergasted. Then he said (to the same clerk) "I'm buying these green peppers." He also allowed himself to be "interviewed" by another clerk who thinks he's the smartest child who ever drew breath. (I know she's silly but I don't interrupt because, heck, nobody ever fussed over my kid before!)

His first grade teacher understood him and his observations amazed her. "I feel I was meant to have him," she wrote in his evaluation. While rehearsing for the class play, Gulliver coached the other children in inflection. His teacher commented, "No first grader ever read with greater expression." When the year was over, his first grade teacher warned his second grade teacher that he was going to change her life forever. She was skeptical, but at the end of that year she wrote, "I am going to miss Gulliver terribly! He's been such an important member of our class. His ideas about the world are amazing and he has grown so in responsibility, social relationships and HANDWRITING! This is a child who defines the best parts of the learning process for me: he's curious, and he loves to share knowledge! What more could one ask for? I will not forget you, Gulliver! Have a great next year. I know you are going to 'wow' them like you did me." His aide, who would no longer be needed, told me, "I simply have to stay in touch because I want to see what he's going to do. I think he is going to be a brilliant scientist."

More e-mail from his first year:

Gulliver is doing UNBELIEVABLY great. Had his IFSP meeting today, and Judith, the goals are all way beyond being met, and the whole staff says they have never seen a child improve so dramatically in such a short time. What's more, they are now fretting about an entirely different issue, namely that of appropriate placement for a gifted/brilliant kid (his teacher says she's never seen a child so advanced in so many areas.) So it's a nice change, wouldn't you say (is my life a roller coaster, or what?) I was thinking last night how startling and marvelous it is, after all the worry and uncertainty, to have ended up with this spirited and glorious and charming child, who delights us every day (even though we have no idea how to approach his education and even though his prodigy predictions are a little scary.) He is just a blast.

This year, for third grade, he qualified for advanced programs in math and reading, and he loves science. He remembers his backpack and lunchbox and he manages transitions, such as changes in seating assignments or schedules, without a problem... mostly. He reads his own fiction compositions when it's time for "author's chair" in the classroom. He feeds the dog and cat and puts his clothes away. Until he was five or six, he didn't want anyone touching his hair. Now he combs his own hair, and brushes his teeth. He gets on an airplane and pops his own ears.

Because his acute sensitivity to sound has diminished, he loves the Fourth of July. He'll try new foods—well, as readily as any child. He plays the piano with perfect pitch, swims, climbs ladders and goes down really scary slides.

The most recent e-mail:

Gulliver's latest report card had a plus mark next to "inferential." This is huge, Judy! He always lagged in his ability to interpret meaning not specifically stated, but he has improved by leaps!!! I am so happy. He still scores "sometimes" in his neatness, his management of tasks, and his distractibility, but he's getting better year by year. He has become a lot more responsible, independent and helpful.

He has such cute ways of expressing himself. Yesterday he said, "I'm feasting on this calculator." He knows "2-to-the-12th-power" by heart, from 2-squared through 12 digits.

Did I tell you about his three-hour dentist visit? He had two cavities fixed... a metal crown and a porcelain one... also some sealant. He did great. He had to go in by himSELF and when he came out the dentist said, "He's REALLY SMART!"

And now Gulliver is nine (or, as he would put it, "9.395 years old.") We are waiting for him to ride a bike and to tie his shoes. We are waiting for him to make a friend. His life is not without challenges, and his behavior still confuses his peers at times. He dislikes social situations ("I don't like all that GREETING!" he says) and eye contact ("It's just hard," he explains.) His voice can be too loud, and he makes annoying repetitive sounds. He has no real grasp of subtle body language or facial expressions. Conversational turn taking remains inconsistent, and he can be unintentionally rude. New things might alarm him. His current fixations—the number 14, asteroids, sticks, ball kicking—are sometimes less than endearing (at least he's over that snake obsession!)

But he smiles at people, and he answers when spoken to. He asks intelligent questions, he devises creative approaches to problems, he takes responsibility for his actions, he remembers things he learns, he apologizes if he hurts someone, and he knows how to build a beautiful fire, kindling to peak.

Best of all, he says, "I love you," unprompted and often, and means it.

One comment from Ms. Bluestone has remained with me throughout each step of this journey. She said, "He will probably always be different, but that doesn't mean he won't be happy or won't make other people happy." In the end, it comes down to that.

And as grateful as we are for the help we received from HANDLE, we embrace, too, what Ms. Bluestone said about the many hurdles Gulliver has surmounted. Who made it happen? His parents? His OT? His SLP? His teachers? Judith?

"I give all the credit to Gulliver," she said. And she was right.

THERE IS NO BLAME
A POSTSCRIPT BY JUDITH BLUESTONE

In several of these stories you have heard the voices of parents who felt betrayed by, or at least not supported by, their children's pediatricians and other service providers. I am sure that these families realize it was not out of calloused disregard that these professionals, who sincerely want to help children attain the basic skills needed for independent lives in society, could not provide them answers. Or offered medication to mask the symptoms when the parents wanted something else or something more. Or inoculated a child against dreaded diseases, not knowing that this particular child had an underlying susceptibility to something in the vaccine. In a true systems approach, there is no blame. We are each doing the best we can at any given time, using the resources available to us.

In the United States in the 21st century, physicians employ tools, usually medication, to deal with isolated symptoms. Teachers have been trained to teach specific subjects and to control behaviors. Yet, neither group has been given the tools or training to understand and help the special children who currently fill their rosters—children who, in growing numbers, struggle with neurodevelopmental disorders more serious than we have seen in previous decades. As some of the families have shared, their children may have been harmed by immunizations. They may be weakened by allergies, by toxins in the environment. They may have nutritional deficits. These are some of the issues doctors and researchers are trying to determine and to resolve. They are not easy. And they are interrelated to the other problems the children demonstrate.

That we all must work together becomes obvious as you read the stories of only a small percentage of the children with CHARGE Syndrome whom HANDLE has helped. There is a place for medical intervention, and nurturing school environments, as well as other complementary therapies as we work collaboratively to help families overcome challenges that seem unreal in their complexity and immensity.

In the final sections of this anthology, you will meet more Churkendeese whose spirit and accomplishments are truly awesome.

PART 5

WHAT ARE YOU, ANYWAY?

—Ben Ross Berenberg
The Churkendoose
Part Chicken, Turkey, Duck and Goose

IT'S JUST A DIFFERENT PLACE
KAREN GINN

Morgan Ginn arrived a month early, in January 1996, thus ending what was an emotionally distressing pregnancy. The previous August, we discovered that we were having twins. Girls! In September, however, we suspected problems. We learned that Taylor's hypoplastic (smaller-than-normal) heart would threaten her life, but believed that Morgan had "only" a cleft lip and palate, and perhaps a "small hole in her heart." Our main concern at their birth was ministering to Taylor and her problems, but Morgan got our attention on her second of day of life. She experienced what the doctors "thought" was a seizure, but I still believe she was bidding our attention because she knew she needed help too. As the doctors began to look more closely at Morgan, they made a diagnosis of CHARGE Syndrome. They told us that Morgan may not walk, talk, see, hear or be mentally capable. Yet, Morgan proves them wrong every day!

CHARGE Syndrome is a relatively rare set of symptoms identified in the early 1980's, of which the causes are yet unknown. Each case is different as the effects of each anomaly can range from mild to severe. CHARGE Syndrome has a variety of physical implications and affects multiple senses. Many children with CHARGE Syndrome are deaf/blind to varying degrees.

CHARGE is an acronym for the collection of anomalies

found in those diagnosed. The "C" of CHARGE stands for coloboma, a cleft-type defect of the eye or optic nerve. Morgan has a cleft on her optic disk, and we were concerned about her vision. Although her acuity had been tested and considered OK, we suspected that her eyes were not working together properly.

"H" is for heart defect. Morgan's was a constriction of the aorta, which was repaired along with a PDA ligation. This is a procedure that closes a duct in the heart that is used by the baby in the womb and normally closes on its own. She now wears a Gore Tex patch on her heart. When she was 12 days old, we kissed her, told her to be careful, and sent her to the operating room at 7 a.m. At 1 p.m., the nurses came to tell us that they were still trying to get a line in. We sat until 7 p.m. that night before they came to tell us that she was coming out of the operating room. I can still see the surgeon walking down the hall to meet us; he was shaking his head, saying, "She was tough on me." He then explained that he had to try three techniques before he got one to work. We also learned later that the nurses did not expect to see her back in the NICU after surgery. But, as we were quick to learn, Morgan showed us that she is very tough and resilient! And this is fortunate, as we are still facing a surgery to place a stent in this narrowed area in the near future. The "small hole in her heart" has repaired itself.

Atresia of the choanae, the "A" of CHARGE, is a narrowing of the opening from the nose to the throat. Morgan actually has choanal stenosis, as her chonae, where the nasal passages meet the pharynx at the end of the hard palate, were not completely closed. She was born with a bilateral cleft lip and palate, which actually was a blessing for her because it allowed her to breathe through her nose.

The "R" of CHARGE represents renal problems.[1] Morgan is missing a kidney and has bladder reflux, which is managed with a preventive antibiotic. "G" is for growth

---

[1] The CHARGE Syndrome Foundation website states that the "R" in CHARGE stands for Retardation of Growth and Development. But, since so many systems are effected, and life is so tenuous, "R" is an effect, not a cause. The "R" word by itself is too harsh for most families to contend with, so, as Morgan's mom, most families find their own "R" word. Morgan's mom actually has taken a part of the "G" in Genito-Urinary Disorders, under which renal irregularities are grouped. But we each protect ourselves in the areas of our greatest vulnerability, so we will allow Morgan's mom her own "R".

problems, and although she is small in stature, at this time we don't believe that Morgan is lacking in growth hormones. Finally, the "E" is for low set, tipped ears, often including abnormalities of the middle and inner ear, which are typical of CHARGE children. Morgan also has bilateral hearing loss and wears aids in both ears. Her vestibular system was compromised, leaving her with very poor balance.

Many CHARGE children have a tendency toward poor muscle tone in their upper body. As a result, feeding and swallowing problems are common. Gastroesophageal reflux (GERD) is also associated with poor muscle tone, and can lead to aspiration pneumonia. Due to Morgan's early swallowing difficulties, she received most of her nutrition through a tube and ate very little orally. As a newborn, she had a nasogastric tube to bring nutrition through her nose to her stomach. At six months, the doctors placed a PEG tube into her abdomen, so that we could feed her directly into her stomach. Morgan's poor swallow still prevents her from eating enough orally to sustain her, but she does like Pringles potato chips and will eat those anytime!

A second surgery at 29 days, to alleviate congenital hydrocephalus, involved inserting a shunt to drain the extra fluid from her head into her abdominal cavity. At age two and a half, Morgan endured another surgery to tighten the top of her stomach. The procedure was successful in easing her gastric reflux by preventing the contents of her stomach from backing up into her esophagus, causing her vomiting and pain. Because the reflux also caused her a great deal of trouble with her ears, chronic ear infections lessened dramatically after the surgery and she could now wear her hearing aids consistently. She began to recognize and make sounds.

Eight major procedures and numerous hospitalizations for tests and illnesses left Morgan with a host of sensory issues. Her hands and feet were very sensitive. She would pull away at the slightest touch, even in her sleep. Yet with all of the blood sticks and tests, this was understandable. Morgan's mouth was also very sensitive. She had undergone surgery to repair her cleft lip and palate, and had been on a ventilator for the first several weeks of her life. She would not allow us to clean her teeth, or even touch her lip area. Her lip muscles were extremely tight and, much to my disappointment, she could not pucker for a kiss. Morgan did not warm to strangers, and was clingy and whiny in new situations.

Bath time was most difficult. When she was very small, we would wash her in the kitchen sink with a shower attachment. When she was big enough for the tub, she would tolerate it, but did not enjoy it. On one occasion, following a hospital stay, she looked up from her spot in the tub and began to scream. She wanted out immediately. It was a long time before we were able to get her to tolerate a bath in the tub again. My only guess is that she thought the showerhead looked like a light in the operating room.

Morgan developed scoliosis. One side of her body was stronger and more developed than the other. Strangely enough, her lower-left body and upper-right body were stronger than their counterparts.

At age three, Morgan started preschool talking very little and walking with a walker or crawling on her knees. I jokingly told her teacher at a meeting that one of her goals was to "walk and talk and run circles around her teacher." Well, in January 2000, just a few weeks shy of Morgan's fourth birthday, I received a call from her school to tell me that Morgan had walked the length and width of the gym by herself! To this day, it brings tears to my eyes and goosebumps to my arms when I think of that phone call. Yet still, Morgan was very unsteady on her feet and preferred to walk only if she could hold my hand on familiar terrain. If she tried to run, it was with stiff legs and she swung her left leg out and around to bring it forward more quickly. Morgan hesitated on stairs, and her physical therapist had worked with her for more than a year on alternating feet up and down stairs.

In her young life, Morgan had seen numerous therapists and caregivers. I had read about The HANDLE Institute on the CHARGE Syndrome listserv, and had met Judith Bluestone at the Indianapolis CHARGE Conference in the summer of 2001. When I learned that Judith would be in Chicago in August, we made an appointment for an evaluation. Since that eventful appointment, Morgan has made great strides physically, socially and mentally.

Our therapy program was designed to enhance Morgan's balance, gait, muscle tone, swallowing and chewing as well as improve her binocular vision and decrease the congestion in her sinus area. The activities were easy to do and we both enjoyed them. Some of the changes in Morgan have been very subtle, and some have been more on the lines of a "Eureka!" Most beneficial was a change in her sleeping habits. She didn't sleep well, always needing to burrow her feet under one of my body parts. If I got up, she'd awaken immediately. Since we began the HANDLE exercises, however, she is more relaxed when she sleeps. Several weeks after we began the exercises, I noticed that she was sleeping on her back, legs straight out and completely relaxed. This was one of those times when I thumped myself on the head and said, "I have never seen her sleep with her legs straight out before!" She still likes to burrow her feet, but it's not necessary. She is less fearful of the dark and we no longer need to leave a hall light on for her. Now, she sleeps alone for a solid ten hours most nights.

Morgan's balance and body awareness have improved tremendously. She runs! Her gait is smoother, and she picks her knees up instead of kicking her feet out to the side. It is so awesome to see her run after her best friend, Alexandria, on the playground. At her big sister's soccer game, we were sitting on the sidelines, and she took off on her own down the hill. I held my breath, as I had never seen her navigate a hill on her own, but she did it! The look on her face, which matched mine, was pure pride.

I looked on with satisfaction as she shifted from one foot to the other in the middle of the living room, practicing steps from her dance class. She has learned to hop on two feet—and actually leave the ground—and she can gallop. At her most recent class, she momentarily stood on one foot with her leg behind her and attempted a "shuffle" tap step! This was not bad for a child who previously used the wall for security to get up on the dance floor, which was just four inches higher than the dressing area floor!

Morgan's sensory issues are improving. It's now difficult to get her out of the bath once she gets in. She loves to pretend she's swimming. Two weeks after beginning the HANDLE exercises, a friend of my husband's came to visit for the weekend. She had never met this man, so I anticipated that she would be very shy and cling to me while he was there. Boy was I wrong! She immediately bonded with him and did not leave his side the entire weekend.

Morgan now tolerates touch quite well, and even offers the next fingernail to be trimmed. And, we now receive very precious, puckered up, noisy kisses from her! Morgan's smile, which was once charmingly lopsided, is becoming

Morgan, *front left*, with her sisters, Makenzie and Kaci at holiday time.

Twinkle, twinkle, little star...

wider and straighter, this, her gift to the family for the 2001 holiday season, and most certainly a result of some of our unique HANDLE activities.

Morgan loves to spin, but prior to our HANDLE program, she seemed not to get dizzy. Her physical and occupational therapists had been trying for a long time to elicit nystagmus, the lingering adjustment of the eyes to tracking the world as it revolves around, through spinning exercises. Well, I am happy to say that Morgan seems to have gotten dizzy for the first time. After a sustained spinning session, Morgan's ears and cheeks became very red, she vomited, then fell asleep, like a person who'd had too much to drink and passed out with the spins. It was only six in the evening. Is it possible that she can now get dizzy? Or, is this the reason she used to vomit excessively? I don't know, but I'm inclined to think that the exercises designed to restore her vestibular system are working!

Judith suggested that we transition Morgan to kindergarten this year. She had attended two years of preschool at a program for deaf/hard of hearing children, and was attending the pre-kindergarten program in our home district. Unfortunately, her pre-kindergarten teacher hastened that move by being non-compliant with Morgan's Individualized Education Plan, but it has proven to be a wise move. Morgan is a very perceptive child and seems to know when people are genuine and have her best interests at heart. Even though I thought pre-kindergarten was the right place for Morgan, she let us know that she could do more and needed to be challenged. The visual exercises Morgan has been performing, such as red/blue glasses and the rolling pin activities, have provided Morgan with the underlying skills she needs to succeed academically. She has picked up reading and writing as well as the average five year old, indicating that her mental abilities and will to learn are outstanding given the tremendous obstacles that she has had to overcome.

Physical issues, such as balance, have improved to the degree that they are no longer important considerations. She and her classmates just have to be a little more careful and more aware of each other on the playground. She continues to make progress with a smaller class size, where her teacher suits her well.

And, I was so proud of her performance at the elementary school Christmas concert. She knew all the words and knew exactly where and when she was supposed to move. I received many, many compliments and words of amazement at how well she did. I knew that she knew the words because she had serenaded me at 6 a.m. every day of our Thanksgiving break! It was precious, but I sure could have used the extra sleep!

Morgan's verbal skills have improved notably. She now uses five and six word sentences consistently and is easier to understand. She answers "why" questions and makes requests for help. People who do not know Morgan well can understand her now, and her speech therapist is impressed with her speech! She cannot believe that a child with a hearing impairment and a cleft can produce such clear speech. Within the first month of her HANDLE exercises, Morgan was able to drink from a straw and move her tongue side to side. She chews a wider variety of foods and swallows more efficiently. Though she may continue to be tube fed for quite some time, she eats more orally than before and can drink a small glass of liquid in a reasonable period.

Throughout our meetings with Judith, I was awed by the connection that she seemed to have with Morgan. Morgan was very cooperative and didn't cling to either me or to our nurse. She was a bit wary, but did not hesitate to engage in the activities under Judith's direction. Following our second session, Judith referred us to our local HANDLE therapist. As we were saying good-bye, with Judith standing a good distance away, Morgan looked at Judith and made eye contact with her. Judith began to walk toward Morgan. Morgan stretched out her arms to hug Judith! Morgan had never ever initiated a hug for anyone other than a family member or her nurse, Brenda. As I write this, tears are streaming down my face. I cannot express how that moved me. I knew I was witnessing something special at that moment. Morgan and Judith have a special bond that I cannot explain and I, too, felt that Judith could feel what I was feeling. I think that is a gift that God has given to Judith in order for her to help special kids like Morgan. I think that Morgan also has that gift, and will use it to help other people.

I realize that even though Morgan may always have physical issues, her will to learn and her mental ability are above average. How else could she learn all these things while teaching me so many lessons? And as I read over this passage I have written, I realize how overwhelming this seems on paper. But, when I look at my Morgan, I see so much... a beautiful little girl who loves and is loved by her parents and her two sisters. A child who can wrap people around her little finger before they even realize it. A child who, despite the dire predictions of our doctors, walks, talks, grows, learns and interacts with us. A child whose smile lights up the room. A child who makes an entire church smile as she walks down the aisle with her sisters. Morgan has enriched my life in so many ways... I cannot say that I am glad she has CHARGE, as I would give anything for her to have an average childhood, but she has taught me patience and perseverance. I have also become a stronger person that is not afraid to seek out answers, and sometimes demand answers. I have become a better teacher for my students, as I am more patient with them and am able to recognize and better understand their difficulties. The following article says it beautifully:

WELCOME TO HOLLAND
EMILY PERL KINGSLEY

I am often asked to describe the experience of raising a child with a disability—to try to help people who have not shared that unique experience to understand it, to imagine how it would feel. It's like this...

When you're going to have a baby, it's like planning a fabulous vacation trip—to Italy. You buy a bunch of guide books and make your wonderful plans. The Coliseum. The Michelangelo David. The gondolas in Venice. You may learn some handy phrases in Italian. It's all very exciting.

After months of eager anticipation, the day finally arrives. You pack your bags and off you go. Several hours later, the plane lands. The stewardess comes in and says, "Welcome to Holland."

"Holland?!?" you say. "What do you mean Holland?? I signed up for Italy! I'm supposed to be in Italy. All my life I've dreamed of going to Italy."

But there's been a change in the flight plan. They've landed in Holland and there you must stay.

The important thing is that they haven't taken you to a horrible, disgusting, filthy place, full of pestilence, famine and disease. It's just a different place.

So you must go out and buy new guide books. And you must learn a whole new language. And you will meet a whole new group of people you would never have met.

It's just a different place. It's slower-paced than Italy, less flashy than Italy. But after you've been there for a while and you catch your breath, you look around.... and you begin to notice that Holland has windmills.... and Holland has tulips. Holland even has Rembrandts.

But everyone you know is busy coming and going from Italy... and they're all bragging about what a wonderful time they had there. And for the rest of your life, you will say "Yes, that's where I was supposed to go. That's what I had planned."

And the pain of that will never, ever, ever, ever go away... because the loss of that dream is a very, very significant loss.

But... if you spend your life mourning the fact that you didn't get to Italy, you may never be free to enjoy the very special, the very lovely things... about Holland.[2]

---

[2] *Welcome to Holland*

129

TELL ME MY GIRL ISN'T SMART!
MARILYN OGAN

K ristin was demonstrating a need for intervention beyond what her occupational and physical therapy sessions were offering her. Both
of the school therapists had been working
with her for over five years on balance and motor skill. We
had seen improvement, but it was apparent that she was
becoming increasingly frustrated.

We had heard much about the HANDLE approach from
other parents of children with CHARGE, and had attended
a conference presentation by Judith Bluestone. We made
the decision to drive our daughter from Indianapolis, Indi-
ana to the Detroit, Michigan area to receive a HANDLE
evaluation.

Prior to our HANDLE assessment, we had begun to
worry about motor control and depth and visual perception,
as Kristin was bumping into things, tripping and falling.
She once walked directly into a tree as she was looking
straight at it and discussing it with her class! Another incident occurred at the fire station. How can a child fall flat
on her face, walking on a level surface, while holding an
adult's hand? She was frequently incurring injuries for
which we could find no explanation.

Our ophthalmologist had told us that the small left reti-
nal coloboma (hole in the eye) "did not effect Kristin's vision
significantly." He felt that her greatest challenges were
astigmatism and acuity, which were being corrected with

glasses. During her HANDLE evaluation, Judith asked Kristin to put on glasses with one red lens and one blue lens, and then identify what color a white object appeared. She could not decide between red and blue. This indicated, we learned, that her eyes were not working well together, and she had not yet established a dominant eye. Consequently, she had difficulty getting a visual fix on where an object was in space before her... until she ran into it.

Judith recommended exercises to strengthen Kristin's eye muscles, help them to coordinate and to train, gently, one eye to stay dominant. We have seen a marked improvement in Kristin's spatial awareness, and her incidence of injury has decreased dramatically since initiating her exercise program.

At the time of Kristin's evaluation, we were desperate over feeding issues and toileting. An exercise I remember another parent raving about was the use of a crazy straw to strengthen all the sphincter muscles in the body, thereby improving, among other things, bladder control. When Judith said that it would be too frustrating for Kristin at that time, I was disappointed, but tried to focus on the things we were doing to help her. There were blowing exercises to help with some of this indirectly, for visual reinforcement and training, and for vestibular function. Judith had said that Kristin would tell us when she is ready for the crazy straw. Well, I'm happy to say that she drinks her three cans of Pediasure through a straw now, and she asks for a straw for every drink. We've noticed, as has her teacher, that although we need to remind her to go, she is doing well at staying dry at school and we are making some headway at home. She is still inconsistent, but she is progressing. I guess the input and the output are pretty tied together in more ways than people think!

One of the more fascinating aspects of her evaluation was Judith's observation of Kristin's walk. At first I was confused at the comment that Kristin was "cutting herself off at the neck," but soon enough I learned that it was based on the fact that Kristin would walk with her big toe elevated off the floor. Interestingly, in the ancient Chinese healing art of reflexology, the big toe corresponds to the brain (and within that, the pituitary,) neck, and mouth-jaw and some sinus areas. Sure enough, these are all areas in which Kristin experiences a good deal of problems. She suffers from environmental allergies, sinus drainage and blockage of the airway. She'd had previous problems with a tracheotomy and various problems swallowing, and relating to the pituitary, Kristin has a growth hormone deficiency.

While walking, Kristin also attempted to keep the area of the foot that relates to throat and tonsils from touching the floor. Before she was two years old, Kristin had her tonsils and adenoids removed, and, at the time of her HANDLE evaluation, she still sometimes pushed on the trach site when swallowing. Along with all of these problems, Kristin is also profoundly deaf. She has misshapen ears, and had had multiple bouts with pneumonia at a tender young age.

During her evaluation, Judith observed that Kristin's left side was universally unorganized. My mother noted that Kristin had always preferred to walk on our right side, placing us on her left. We feel that Kristin realized that by placing us on her left, she was forcing her left side to be organized, while feeling secure in the knowledge that we were there as a safeguard in case a problem arose. Tell me my girl isn't smart!

At the time of our evaluation, Kristin had been receiving physical therapy for more than four years. The therapist had been trying to get her to skip and gallop correctly for the last two of those four years. Within the first few weeks of beginning her HANDLE program, Kristin began skipping —*everywhere*! She loves to skip and she now runs with a more even gait.

The HANDLE exercises have given Kristin the skills and confidence to participate fully in soccer; an activity that she will be able to enjoy for years. On picture day in the spring of 2000, Kristin couldn't balance with one foot on the ball and her hands on her hips long enough for the photographer to snap a photo. I posed her and stood behind her until the photographer was ready. When I stepped back, Kristin just wilted and went to her knees. And it wasn't even a very "tall" kneel.

In the fall of 2001, however, we saw her with hands on hips, one foot on the ball and one on the ground. And she was standing so straight, for so long, even as the photographer got distracted for a moment!

At eight years old, and prior to her HANDLE program, Kristin played soccer in a group of four to six year olds due to her poor balance and because we were fearful the larger kids would hurt her. At first, Kristin would be doing well just to move in the general direction of the ball. This past fall season, however, she ran after the ball, fighting to get in a good kick. And she was so thrilled when she did it. She would kick the ball and, using American Sign Language, sign, "Hurray!" and, "Kick good!" This spring, we will be moving her up to the next playing level with six to nine year olds. We feel that because of the progress she's made, Kristin can now play at a more age appropriate level.

It has been nothing short of amazing to discover what we have discovered about Kristin. The HANDLE approach to therapeutic intervention for Kristin's vestibular functioning, tactility, muscle tone, proprioception and visual functioning has been only beneficial. And the exercises require no real expensive or specialized equipment, and a minimal time commitment outside of everyday activities. Most can be done while doing something else. The school's therapists were very interested in the therapy program developed for Kristin, and have incorporated some of the activities into her routine. With the carryover from home to school, the therapies have been paying off great dividends in Kristin's understanding of her world, her ability to make adjustments to it, and in helping her overcome some of her problems.

Kristin's brother, Kenny, is three years older than Kristin. Because he was around for all the "scary medical stuff," he has always been sensitive and very protective of his sister (and other children who might be "different," for whatever reason.) When Ken was 11years old and Kristin was eight, it dawned on Kenny that Kristin was trying to manipulate him into doing many things for her. This was around the time of her evaluation with Judith. One day, he decided he'd had enough of playing fetching-boy and put his foot down, telling her to do it herself. A huge ruckus ensued because Kristin wasn't getting her way. Finally, I stepped into the fray and helped Kristin accomplish what she wanted while Kenny went his merry way.

Well, just yesterday, I had to scold Kristin for being lazy and not getting the stepstool to reach something off the shelf. She and Kenny had fussed over this very same thing just last year. In response, Kristin began dragging over her rocking chair. Needless to say, I explained that was not a very safe option! Kenny then proceeded to lay down the law to her as well. Kristin just looked at him, said he's not her boss and stomped her foot. That's right! She had enough balance not only to stand on one leg for a short time, but also to apply force with her other foot. Don't let anyone tell you that sibling rivalry accomplishes nothing! What I wouldn't have given, just two years ago, to see that little foot stomp!

Postscript, three months later: Kristin is eating now! We are thrilled and amazed. She is no longer on a night drip, she drinks three cans of Pediasure orally during the day and she is on a jelly and bread kick; four slices a day with grape jelly! She can eat well-cut spaghetti, macaroni & cheese and some meats. She loves steak, adores green beans, cooked carrots, and peas!

Yesterday, a co-worker commented, "Kristin was pretty stagnant until you went to Detroit wasn't she? Hasn't she improved a bunch since then?" I thought it interesting that she recognized Kristin's improvement simply by the stories I related at work.

And now, I just have to brag about something Kristin did at soccer practice, which totally caught me by surprise. At her first practice, they played a game of "sharks and minnows" where the "sharks" in the middle try to kick the balls out of bounds. The "minnows" try to get their ball from one line to the other side of the field without having it kicked out. Kristin likes this game, but when the coach said they were going to play the game "with a twist," I got interested. The twist was that the game was to be played while "crab walking." I was concerned because I wasn't sure she had the upper body strength for the crab walk, but she did it! I was stunned. She only had two little dirt spots on her shorts, meaning her little butt didn't slide along the ground to do the activity. And she had so much fun! I know that HANDLE has contributed to these successes.

A REVOLUTION HAS HAPPENED
BARBARA GRAVES

The geneticist who confirmed that Benjamin has Down's Syndrome was terribly wrong when he said that he would be nothing more than a "docile puppy dog." Ben has a mind of his own and he is determined to get what he wants, one way or another. When we were slow in getting him a boat ride, he got himself on a boat... three different times. Ben's current passion is to ride a horse, and to have one of his own someday. I have no doubt that, somehow, both will happen.

For a long time, Benjamin was small. We could simply pick him up and tote him. And we did, far longer than we did his five older siblings, and far past the age we should have. When he misbehaved, we changed his location and found him something new, as we might have done with a preschool child. Consequently, he was slow to learn to take verbal instruction. Now, at nearly ten, our challenge is to get him to comply with verbal requests when he has a different agenda. Life with Benjamin has never been boring, but it is frequently challenging.

To put my mind back into Benjamin's first nine years is difficult. We've been so focused on keeping him occupied in the moment that we seldom have time for reflection. And so, I draw from the notes I made in preparation for Ben's HANDLE evaluation to give you a sense of Ben:

Ben prefers group activities to solitary ones and he has

always been very social. The people he counts among his friends are far more numerous than the ones who ignore him. Although he has no trouble with adults and older kids, developing relationships with kids his own age is hard because he doesn't understand the etiquette of boundaries and social distance. Although he craves social contact, he hasn't figured out how to get it positively. It is easy for him to get caught up in roughhouse play, and then he has difficulty exiting from it. Sometimes it takes physical restraint to get him to stop.

At school, Ben's focus wanders. In fact, all aspects related to his attentiveness are problems: completing tasks, accepting change and transitions, sitting still, following directions. His teachers and therapists need to pull upon all of their creative energy to keep him engaged, particularly with academic and small motor activities. Ben can be impulsive, and his behavior is unpredictable. Interestingly, though, he has an "orderly" streak. Although most of Ben's therapists love to work with him, they find him a challenge.

The school staff blames "mental retardation" for Ben's lack of academic success; I think the school situation lacks appropriate teaching strategies. The school staff attributes his acting-out to poor training at home; we think the behaviors are due to lack of respect for him in the school situation. The behaviors diminish when school is not in session.

Generally, we need to rock Ben to sleep. In the darkness, it is worse. To stay asleep, he needs another person in bed with him. He breathes through his mouth, grinds his teeth and bites his fingernails. He also seems to have problems with heat regulation, and he prefers his baths cold. He complains about having his nails cut or his hair trimmed, and he doesn't like to brush his teeth or wash his hands.

But, Ben loves sports, especially ball sports, and he will play for hours. Even though his balance is poor, and he has a tendency to bump into things, he skateboards and rollerblades. Once he starts on an activity, such as swinging, spinning or jumping, he doesn't want to stop. And he can't seem to sustain his stride when he runs; he loses his synchronicity after half a block, and has to stop to regroup. Yet, Ben somehow seems to need this movement and the activity.

Armed with these notes about Ben's behavior, he and I entered into his HANDLE evaluation in December 2000. His sense of humor endeared him to Judith Bluestone and

Marlene Suliteanu, who conducted his evaluation. When Marlene flipped backward in the legless rocking chair, Ben laughed and laughed. Thereafter, Ben delighted in reminding everyone of the "rocking chair incident."

Judith and Marlene identified Ben's weak systems: tactility, muscle tone, proprioception, kinesthesia and ocular motility. They observed that Ben relied heavily on his auditory system, yet his auditory sequencing was weak. This made auditory activities, such as counting, challenging, and helped explain why Ben had difficulty remembering and executing verbal instruction. They also noticed that in tasks demanding fine motor coordination, Ben's tongue, toes and even his whole body became active, thus hampering the development of his fine motor skills.

Judith and Marlene helped me to understand that Ben expressed himself better than we had been giving him credit for, except he did it with his body, rather than with words. When Ben crawled under the table to avoid paper and pencil work, Judith responded in kind to Ben's non-verbal communication; she followed Ben under the table. This, of course, delighted Ben and the two pretended the space was an oven. When they were "thoroughly baked," Ben popped out of the oven and returned to the table to continue with the evaluation.

And then came the therapy plan: movement activities, tapping stimulations, HANDLE massage techniques, reflexology and dietary recommendations. I must admit that we weren't able to do everything consistently as our household was in turmoil due to a move, but Ben has achieved many significant gains.

Within a few months, Ben's language improved, including his word retrieval, articulation and pronunciation. Where once he could barely stand to hold a pencil or perform any fine motor task, he is now able to trace letters. Nine months later, I watched him lace four cardboard cars with shoestrings, one after another in a period of 10 minutes. He can sit at a table without falling out of his chair, and focus for 10 to 15 minutes on paper and pencil tasks. As recently as a couple of months ago, he would have thrown the work on the floor.

Ben is running cross-country and recently started Saturday Soccer. At school, I watched as he ran around the gym in a fluid run and as he played tag on the playground for two fifteen-minute periods without once hitting someone too hard. Ben can now skip back and forth across the gym and do a cartwheel with his legs over his head in the proper rotation. He can hug without squeezing too tight, and let go at the appropriate moment.

HANDLE therapy has changed the way we see Benjamin, and it has given him new options. This year, we placed Benjamin in a regular fourth grade class. It is the scariest, most surreal thing that I have ever done, but every day Ben comes up to the plate in a new way. We are supporting him with pull-out sessions, curricular adaptations, a machine to facilitate communication and 15 minutes of exercise for every hour he is in class. I have done the fourth grade reading and math with him at home. Although he does it grudgingly, he does it with capacity. A revolution has happened, and I think that perhaps Benjamin's body has settled down enough to study.

I don't remember the Benjamin from a year ago. I can tell you about the progress of other people's children. I can see last week to this week. But, I can see that last year I thought that he had no intellectual life. This year, I can't believe I ever felt that way.

CUTTING AN ELEPHANT IN HALF DOES NOT PRODUCE TWO SMALL ELEPHANTS
A POSTSCRIPT BY JUDITH BLUESTONE

When Morgan's and Kristin's families learned so early that their baby girls had multiple impairments that required medical intervention, they were relieved to know that specialists in various arenas were well trained and available to implement life-saving surgeries and other procedures. They required all the support the hospitals and rehabilitation services could provide so their little girls had a chance to live and to grow into their maximal capability. But once children, or adults, achieve stable medical condition and concerns turn to those of developmental functions, doctors are usually not the people best equipped to guide treatment, other than to determine the parameters of treatment to ensure medical safety and well-being.

Parents need resources when their special needs children, even those with genetic disorders such as CHARGE Syndrome or Down's Syndrome, plateau behaviorally for more than two or three months. In Morgan's case, her sleep patterns certainly indicated something irregular. Medication to help her sleep would only mask the symptoms. Morgan's problem with sleep stemmed largely from insecurity with her body-in-space. If, with her eyes closed, she could not tell where she was, she needed to burrow under someone else to make sure she was not falling out of bed or floating off in space, perceptually, of course. Ironic, isn't it, that her eyes were giving her misinformation when she was in motion, but they were necessary to support proprioceptive security? And so bathing (closing her eyes if water splashed on her face) and sleeping were not comfortable events for her. What was the underlying deficit? That sluggish vestibular system, of course! The underpinning of muscle tone, visual tracking and proprioception.

So to whom would Morgan's parents and Kristin's parents turn for help with their children's problems? Ophthalmologists, eye doctors who determine the health and structural fitness of the eye, should certainly be the first to see a child with colobomas or other physical abnormality of the visual system, such as those involved in CHARGE. However, visual functions, such as binocular teaming and accommodations (change of focus from near-point to far), visual tracking, and certainly visual perception fall into the domain of another expert.

Developmental or Behavioral Optometrists are the doctors best suited for determining concerns related to visual functions. In the late 1960's and early 1970's, I frequently worked collaboratively with "granddaddies" of developmental optometry—Dr. Tom Rose and Dr. Elliot Forrest, in Ohio and New York, respectively. My role was to add activities of the whole body that nurtured the supports to various visual functions—to develop the perceptual-motor basis tie-in that would provide the brain the ability to develop perceptual constancy of a whole system so visual gains would be faster in coming and stable once developed. In this collaborative work, I, too, learned much about the visual system, to embellish what I had already learned from the inside-out from my own unusual visual processing problems.

It was fortunate that I had refreshed my understanding of visual functions by meeting with a study group of developmental optometrists in the northwest as part of the Optometric Extension Program. I could not only understand what Kristin's ophthalmologist had found, I also knew that with red-blue lenses I could help Kristin's binocular perception. And I knew from my holistic approach how to integrate Kristin's weak systems so she could gain the three-dimensional perspective that would provide sense to the proprioceptive messages she was receiving via the tactile system of proprioceptive receptors at her joints. And I knew that by strengthening her muscle tone through the special Peacemaker Massage, we could build a stronger base for balance, while bypassing those areas of her damaged inner ear that could not play a part in helping her develop body-in-space and general balance.

Had we continued to "cut Kristin in half," that is, allowed the ophthalmologic verdict to stand, and worked only on the end-point activity of balance for balance sake, Kristin most likely would still not be able to have her soccer picture taken without something propping her to stand. We are each systemic in our functions, and this cannot be overlooked, even, or perhaps especially, when dealing with individuals with rare syndromes.

CHARGE Syndrome and Down's Syndrome have little in common it would seem. They certainly result from different genetic abnormalities. Yet they have more commonality than differences. Human structure and function are more alike in all of us than they are different from one of us to another.

So, Ben, whose muscle tone was too weak to support proper gait, especially in running, also had diminished muscle tone that interfered with his ability to articulate his ideas clearly. Ben's slow response time and poor endurance for large and fine motor tasks, and his difficulty in expressing himself verbally, led others to believe his mental capacity was limited. This is so frequently the case with children and adults with Down's. But once the therapy stops focusing on gait and writing and speech, but rather on muscle tone and the neurodevelopmental underpinnings of muscle tone, then the body strengthens itself through a unity among the senses.

The brain's primary function, after all, is to make order out of chaos, and it does that by developing perceptual constancy. It requires multiple simultaneous stimulation to create the energy that signals different areas of the brain that enough coherent information exists among different parts of the body to indicate to the brain that an event is important and must be organized and retained. This is the beauty of a systems approach—a holistic approach—to neurodevelopment, and how it really does yield learning efficiency. It builds perceptual patterns within the brain.

It can do this even for children whose brains have been damaged prior to birth; those who have never experienced this world as most others do. HANDLE has help for many of the problems with which they entered life, even after they reach adulthood.

PART 6

I CAN'T WALK, I WOULDN'T TAKE THE CHANCE, BUT IF YOU GIVE ME SOME MUSIC, I'LL GO INTO MY DANCE

—Ben Ross Berenberg
The Churkendoose
Part Chicken, Turkey, Duck and Goose

NOTHING TO LOSE
DON AND MARY

Holly came into our lives on a snowy night in December 1997, fourteen weeks before her due date and weighing just 860g, (less than two pounds.) Her identical twin, Grace, had died in utero three weeks earlier.

The traumatic weeks and months that followed should have, but didn't, prepare us for the medical assessment we were given in September 1998; Holly was diagnosed with Cerebral Palsy. All four of her limbs were affected.

Months later, and despairing of the limited and ineffectual state services available in Cork, Ireland, our local physiotherapist introduced us to HANDLE. We were immediately impressed with the philosophy and ethos of the HANDLE approach. The emphasis was not on expensive equipment or on exercise for the sake of exercise. We were taken with the concept of developing Holly's potential in a holistic, non-intrusive manner. We had nothing to lose— Holly was now sixteen months old, but had no head control, high muscle tone and pronounced spasticity. It was time to follow our gut instinct and try the practical, common sense HANDLE way.

Holly adapted to the HANDLE programme with ease—no doubt helped by the fact that she got on so well with her HANDLE friend, Cathy Stingley (or "Cappy" as she calls her.) She didn't have to do things she didn't want to do. The "less is more" philosophy meant that she wasn't being stressed... and neither were we!

Cathy suggested introducing Yoga to the programme and we now credit many of Holly's improvements to the complementarity of Yoga to the HANDLE approach.

And how has Holly progressed over the past three years?

First, she is a bright, happy and friendly child with a wicked sense of humour—how much of this is attributable to HANDLE is a moot point! But Holly has improved noticeably...

...she is much more flexible and has just about begun to roll a little

...she has taken to her walker like the proverbial duck to water

...she can differentiate her left from her right with ease and knows all her body parts—very important for getting those brain patterns functioning properly

...she can sit cross-legged for minutes at a time, unsupported

...she is making huge efforts to feed herself

...and, of course, she could talk the hind legs off a donkey.

We're not claiming (and we'd be pretty sure that neither Judith nor Cathy would claim) that HANDLE, on its own, has brought Holly this far. But the HANDLE approach and programme have been hugely important in developing her abilities to the maximum, particularly during those crucially important formative years.

At this stage, Holly is looking forward to going to a very welcoming mainstream school next September. For us, also, it will be a milestone—one that HANDLE has helped to achieve.

WHO KNOWS WHAT THE FUTURE HOLDS?
EMILY DAVIS

I thank God for HANDLE! I am a 25-year-old woman with Cerebral Palsy (CP). To truly understand how miraculous HANDLE has been in my life, I must share with you my past, then you will begin to understand my present.

Initially, I came to HANDLE because I was having difficulty learning to drive using hand controls. When I would try to use the hand controls, which requires each hand to perform a different task, I found myself in a traumatic situation. If I wanted to turn the car, I'd break out in a cold sweat because getting my muscles to turn the wheel and press the accelerator at the same moment was so stressful.

Over the years, I have learned that my body is wired uniquely. It's as though my nerves are connected directly to *every* muscle. To move one part of my body meant that *all* of the other muscles were working too. Even when I would talk, I could feel muscle tension increase in my legs.

Throughout my life, I was told there really wasn't much to be done except preserve the capabilities that I had. Oh, really?

There are some things that happen, that change us in inconceivable ways, that are hard to believe and even harder to explain. Do you know the capabilities of your body? I thought I did... until this year.

I have felt changes in my body that were once unimaginable! My knees used to be extremely tight and stiff. I am now able to straighten them almost completely. I couldn't raise my hands above my head, and now I can, effortlessly. I recently ordered a walker. I haven't used one in 10 years! It's as if my joints have been oiled and now have the freedom to move as they were intended.

I am a different person because of HANDLE. Each day is an adventure. Driving is difficult, but it's becoming easier because I am dealing with the traditional challenges of driving and no longer struggling so much with my muscle and brain connections. *Incredible*!

During my HANDLE evaluation, I mentioned several difficulties I had been dealing with for years, although truthfully, I didn't expect any assistance in those areas. I talked about my light sensitivity, visual tracking, perception problems and balance issues.

But, the changes in my eyes are amazing! It used to be that I could feel my eyes switching when I would look at something, similar to the change of a camera lens or view. Now, I no longer struggle with having to re-focus every time I look away. And my depth perception continues to improve.

My muscles have started to work individually. This is absolutely astounding! My life is so much easier. I am generally calmer and more relaxed. I could never have anticipated what miraculous changes my body and mind have undergone, and I am shocked at all of the things I can do now that were simply impossible before HANDLE.

My life will never be the same because of HANDLE.

Something incredible has begun to happen! Who knows what the future holds for me?

TRUE CAPABILITIES
MARY CLANCY

Early in Rebecca's development, we were dismissed as over-anxious; parents who would not accept that their child was average. Ultimately, we became parents of a child for whom the professionals had given up. Our fifteen-year-old daughter, Rebecca, has been diagnosed with somodyspraxia, epilepsy and severe food allergies. Her needs are complex.

In February 1998 in Forrest Row, England, I saw Judith Bluestone's conference presentation, "The Art of the Possible." I was impressed with Judith's sincerity. Because she'd known the pain of rejection, she could identify with those she helped. And I knew, immediately, that the HANDLE approach was one that could help Rebecca.

At this time, however, we had previously committed to beginning another programme of exercises under different supervision. When I spoke with Judith about the situation, she told me not to worry. She didn't presume that only she held the answers. She suggested that we begin the other programme, and when the time was right, we should contact The HANDLE Institute. This did not occur until two years later, in April 2000.

As the date for Rebecca's assessment approached, we were apprehensive. Rebecca does not participate, and she does not show the skills that we know she possesses. The HANDLE assessment, however, was a revelation. HANDLE practitioner, Cathy Stingley, and Intern, Linda Salisbury, provided these observations of Rebecca's assessment:

Rebecca entered the front door of the building holding onto her father. Her eyes roamed continually in every direction, never settling on one object for more than a fraction of a second. She clung tightly as she slowly climbed the stairs, sometimes missing a step, each foot coming to rest next to the other before attempting the next step.

In the assessment room, while her eyes continued their constant roam, Rebecca was invited to sit in the best seat in the house, the office swivel chair. Her great difficulties with motor planning became ultimately clear; she could not find the chair unless she faced it, and then she could not manage her body to seat herself. Verbal instructions only caused confusion. With help, she was backed up to the chair, told to sit, hesitated, then fell into it with a plop.

As Linda Salisbury and Judith Bluestone began to get acquainted with Rebecca, they waited patiently as she processed information and laboriously formed her words to respond. Her parents often stepped in to answer for her, until Judith and Linda let them know they were okay with waiting. It gave them information about Rebecca's need to process and the effort it took to produce her halting language. Rebecca, in fact, seemed delighted to be given the response time she needed, and to be validated for what she could do, rather than be judged for what she could not.

Rebecca performed a good deal of the work from the floor, as too much of her attention was focused on the sheer act of sitting—as difficult for her as perching on top of a telephone pole for most people. The first activity introduced to Rebecca was a tracing activity. After an effort to hold the pencil in a primitive grasp, she proceeded to scribble across the page. Enough was observed. She was not asked to do another task requiring a pencil. But she did tell Linda and Judith that she wanted to learn to write.

Linda asked Rebecca to point to her own nose. Rebecca's arms wandered around in the air describing large arcs out from her body. She managed, after some effort, to point to Linda's nose because it was the one she could see, and therefore the only one she thought existed, indicating a profound lack of awareness of her own body. When Rebecca was asked to touch her back, again, her arms parted the air, but no contact was made with her own body. Later we learned that when looking at herself in a mirror, she would

149

touch her features in the mirror, but not her own physical features as she could not relate to them in that way.

Throughout the second part of the assessment, Rebecca was shown a series of flash cards with drawings, the cards displayed for her for a mere fraction of a second. Then, other activities were performed before she was asked to identify what she saw from a selection of four drawings. The figures on the cards became increasingly complicated, but to the astonishment of her parents, Rebecca identified each one of them correctly! They could not imagine how that could be when her eyes never came to rest on any given object.

Through Judith's warm encouragement, Rebecca thrived in the assessment, and Judith became the first person to see her true capabilities. Rebecca demonstrated that she can read when the words are presented very quickly and she is not asked to repeat them immediately. She needed time to process.

Judith was able to answer so many questions that other professionals had been unable to answer. For the first time, we left an assessment feeling positive. Judith gave us proof that Rebecca had the capacity to learn; now we had to unblock the correct neurological pathways and let the information flow.

When we first understood that Judith and Cathy Stingley were based in America, we worried about how we would be able to keep in contact. But our wonderful intern, Linda, sees us through our HANDLE programme. At each review, Linda fine-tunes our exercises to accommodate Rebecca's improvements. We never feel hurried, and I have the sense that we are moving along a continuum of progress, where exercises are refined and customized according to Rebecca's unique needs. From the beginning, we were taught that exercises done under stress are not worth doing. If, on any given day, we were not able to manage the full programme of exercises, we did what we could.

Rebecca's father, John, has given up his full time job, and works only part time, in order to support Rebecca in her programme. Initially, three volunteers assisted John with Rebecca's exercises. Six weeks in, however, Rebecca was able to do the exercises, with the exception of the wrist/ankle rotation, with only John to assist. At our most recent assessment, it was wonderful to watch Rebecca take a lead role in independently carrying out her exercise programme.

Prior to beginning her HANDLE programme, Rebecca could not use her mouth to blow. With the help of the crazy straw exercise, she was able to do so within a week. Within six weeks, we began noticing some very significant developments. Notably, Rebecca's powers of observation had improved and she was beginning to think far more independently. She was demonstrating greater dexterity, and had begun to effectively plan and execute her movements. Her eye control improved and she was able, for the first time, to look at people directly. Linda Salisbury reflects:

One of the early memories I have of Rebecca is her inability to hold eye contact because her eyes were busy telling her the whereabouts of her body. At a later review, Rebecca and I sat and looked at each other, smiling, me not believing the difference and, I expect, Rebecca thinking "Oh, that's what Linda looks like."

Seven months later, Rebecca's posture was better. She was more aware of her body; she could tell what she was feeling, "where it hurt", and the sensation of being hot or cold. For the first time, Rebecca could do a puzzle by herself and she was making progress with letter recognition. Rebecca watches the television news and engages in discussions, using well-founded arguments, of current events. She followed the Presidential election, and explained to her father the decisions of each court and the issues involved.

And now, in early 2002, Rebecca has mastered all of the letters, can pick them out in regular sized print and is beginning to read. She capably and consistently recognizes the numbers one through 10, and she is generalizing ideas. The concept of passing time is no longer a mystery. She knows, for example, on what day of the week December ends, or when it is afternoon.

Rebecca's language is superb, and she is witty and funny. At a recent social dinner for seven, Rebecca participated in our conversation expertly. She enjoys music, learns lyrics quickly and anticipates the rhyming lines in a song she has never heard before.

The coloured Irlen lenses that Rebecca now wears have brightened her world. She now comments on the weather as she is seeing the subtle changes in the sky and the light. And the lenses seem to have stopped what remained of the involuntary motions of her eyes.

At last, Rebecca has selected a dominant hand, the left, and just a few days ago, she spontaneously used a fork to eat her eggy bread—without prompting and with perfect control. Upon request, she can point accurately to a specific picture. Using her index finger is something that she couldn't do just a few months ago. And recently, she received a certificate from a regular gym club for trampolining! She's mastered the "seat drop" and is working on a "quarter turn."

Reports from Rebecca's physiotherapist, speech therapist and teachers all praise HANDLE, and now each incorporates the HANDLE ways into their work with Rebecca. Recently added to her HANDLE programme are exercises to help her gain control of her fingers as a foundation to writing.

Still, school can be stressful, and she is still fairly dependent, but Rebecca has demonstrated great bravery and passion in forging into these unknown areas. She still has a long way to go, but we are miles from where we began. And we are confident in her ability to continue progressing and improving. We are most grateful to those of The HANDLE Institute for our progress to date and for their continued support.

ONE MOM'S OPINION
ANN POTTER

We came to HANDLE when Caitlin was eight and a half years old. It had become apparent that Caitlin, who had started in the traditional system of physical and occupational therapy at 18 months old, needed something more.

Caitlin has undiagnosed neurological delay. She does not walk or talk or feed herself. She has been labeled mentally retarded. Sensory integration has always been a problem for her, but has been treated as a side concern by conventional medicine.

We met with Judith Bluestone for about four and a half hours on that first day and left with an entirely new approach to Caitlin's multiple problems. First, I, Caitie's mother, had been missing *a lot* of Caitie's cues. Over the years, the family had learned Caitie's particular method of communication, and yet I found out in one afternoon that we had been missing many, many of the subtle clues that she had been giving us. From the very beginning, Judith spoke to Caitlin as though Caitie could understand everything, and then *waited* for a response. It became obvious that Caitlin could understand much more than I had dared to hope, but she needed a little more time to process her response than she was usually given.

Secondly, traditional therapies we've used have tended to override signals from Caitlin in attempting to make her

"learn" specific tasks. For example, if Caitie resisted standing with only one hand on the wall, the tendency for the
therapist was to "push through" the fear until Caitie could
do it. Judith, on the other hand, looked at Caitie and said,
"She has little or no depth perception, little muscle control,
and decreased proprioception. She's scared because her
body is not ready for this step. Let's listen to her body language and strengthen her nervous system before asking her
to do something she's ill-equipped to do."

So we worked, and still work, on her nervous system.
We do tapping exercises on her head and face; we do sensory integration exercises; we do vestibular exercises. We
do many of the same things traditional therapies do with
one exceedingly important difference—*we listen to Caitlin*.
Trips to the physical therapist when Caitlin was three had
proved so traumatic that after two months we gave up. After eight months of daily HANDLE work, Caitie and I still
have *fun* when we do "our" exercises.

The bottom line results? Caitie quit drooling within the
first week of the exercises. Within about four months, her
sleep apnea noticeably improved. Her back is straighter for
longer periods. Caitie now routinely crawls over to the piano and plays from a kneeling position until I put her in a
chair. She loves the piano and will sit for 30 to 45 minutes,
stick straight, to play it. This is a new event since beginning
the HANDLE program.

Although she doesn't yet talk, Caitie has a much greater
range of noises and "songs" than she used to, including
"singing" the first half of "do, re, mi." On a whim one day, I
decided to use Caitie's interest in music to see if she would
pay attention to "Hooked on Phonics." She loved it and can
distinguish A, B, and C from a random group of numbers.
We are working on learning the alphabet at home.

During the first six months of working with HANDLE, I
pulled Caitie out of school so her only therapy was that of
HANDLE. Thus, all of these successes are attributable
solely to HANDLE.

We are now back "in the system" at school. I have come
to believe that Caitlin's best opportunity lies in incorporating HANDLE's techniques and *mindset* into her traditional
classroom setting. She needs the interaction with other
children, she needs the chance to use her walker, and she
needs the opportunity to make choices within a structured
setting. Most importantly, she needs the guidance of *some-*

one other than her mother, which is why I am so thankful to Caitie's teacher and physical therapist for being willing to incorporate the HANDLE techniques into her school program. I *strongly believe* that if we had been able to use the HANDLE approach in conjunction with traditional therapies when Caitie was one or two, rather than eight and a half years old, she would have been walking and talking long ago.

Most importantly, if no another accomplishment were achieved, I would be forever grateful to HANDLE for teaching us to *listen to Caitie.* The stress reduction in my child is noticeable, and best of all, communication has never been better.

If you are a teacher, therapist or aide in special services, I beg you to listen to the HANDLE ideas with an open mind and to bring them back to your classrooms. The ideas are based on the fact that a child's behavior gives us a clue as to the needs of the child and shouldn't be overridden. They are based on strengthening specific neural pathways. The techniques are gentle and non-intrusive for the child. We all have nothing to lose and everything to gain from trying HANDLE.

THE HUMAN SPIRIT
A POSTSCRIPT BY JUDITH BLUESTONE

I sn't the human spirit amazing! Little Holly already "talking the hind legs off a donkey," and Emily having the courage to break barriers that others assume are permanent. And Rebecca, who can finally find her own nose and see the world and those in it without falling over! All it took was a little guidance on a program that was neurodevelopmentally correct for each of these brave Churkendeese.

How lucky for Rebecca that a teacher at her school could help guide her HANDLE program and share most of its principles and practices with others on Rebecca's team. Her story, along with Kristin's and Leah's, let us know that Ann Potter's plea for schools to recognize HANDLE is not an unrealistic cry. Schools can incorporate much of what HANDLE has to teach, and they can start by understanding the wisdom of Gentle Enhancement and by seeing what behaviors are telling us, rather than stifling the behaviors that they find bothersome. If the stories so far have not reinforced those basic tenets, perhaps the stories of Nick and Austin, that follow, will provide the convincing evidence.

PART 7

MAKING FRIENDS CAN BE A PLEASURE

—Ben Ross Berenberg
The Churkendoose
Part Chicken, Turkey, Duck and Goose

THEN THERE WAS NICK'S...
TERRY V.

Nicholas was fussy in the beginning. Born just eleven months after my marriage, at age 21, it was difficult to tell if his fussiness made me a nervous young mother, or if my nervousness made him a fussy youngster. Yet, he grew into a happy, healthy, energetic baby and toddler. He loved to sing and play; the more activity we cooked up, the happier he was.

But by the time Nick entered Kindergarten I began noticing little "quirks" in his personality. Maybe I was more attuned to these things because my brother suffered from Tourette's Syndrome, a disorder characterized by repeated involuntary movements and/or vocal sounds called tics. The last thing I wanted was to become a paranoid mother, concerned with every eye blink, grimace or gesture. Yet, I was concerned. My brother's research on Tourette's suggested that it was an inherited disorder.

As Kindergarten progressed, I asked Nick's teacher to keep me informed of any behavior that seemed out of the ordinary and she assured me that he was well liked and enthusiastic. On Parents' Night my husband and I were eager to see the results of his first full school year's work. We looked at his classmates' writings, drawings and colorings, all neat and complete. Then there was Nick's... We could tell by looking at his work that he was rushing through projects, probably anxious to move on to something else. Yet his report card showed all good marks.

This trend continued through the first couple of years of elementary school. His teachers praised his knowledge and competence. At home, he was a whirling dervish, as if he had a day's worth of pent up energy bursting to come out. And I began to notice tics. He would pull at his eyelashes, stretch his face as if he were yawning, and rub his eyes incessantly. He would stand while watching television, shifting his weight from one foot to the other, repeating the dialogue.

As his homework increased, so did my frustration. We spent hours every night at the table trying to complete the day's simple assignments. He certainly had the knowledge; he lacked the ability to sit still and focus. He would continually drop his pencil, pick it up, lie upside down on the chair, go look out the window, pet the cat, get a snack—anything but concentrate on the task at hand. I would either leave the room in tears, or finish the assignment myself just to get it over with.

It was around this time that I sought professional help for his problem. We consulted with a pediatric neurologist, a supposed expert in the field of behavioral problems. After listening to my story and spending a few minutes of observation alone with him, she diagnosed him with Tourette's Syndrome and ADHD. I cried as she informed me of her findings. Whether they were tears of sorrow for what he might have to face, or tears of joy at having a name for his problem at last, I don't know. She wanted to start him on Ritalin immediately. I had heard stories of this alleged wonder drug, and refused to subject him to the side effects. Then she suggested a drug called Clonadine, which is used to treat patients with high blood pressure. She suggested that this would calm him down and help him focus, though she warned that it could worsen his tics. We started him on a low dosage.

His usually rosy cheeks became pale. His bright eyes dimmed. He'd fall asleep soon after taking his daily dose. I'd watch him sleeping, my once vibrant, happy boy, and I'd think, "Am I doing this for you or for me?"

Fifth grade began, and we were finally fortunate to have him under the care of a genuinely concerned teacher. She would write notes home on his behavior or call if there was something out of the ordinary—even if it was to say he was having a good day. It seemed that as the day progressed and the previous night's medication wore off, he'd lose his grip. Every night I'd get the same awful, guilty feeling as I watched him drift off to sleep after taking his medication.

That same school year, I was fortunate to be working only part-time and was able to help at the school. I noticed a line of kids forming outside of the nurse's office at lunchtime to take their various medications. I noticed that many of the prescriptions were for Ritalin. I couldn't help but think about all of these "junkies"—kids with real problems, being given pills just to get them through their day!

Thankfully, through a desperate hope to find a cure for his Tourette's, my brother found The HANDLE Institute's website on the internet. He had been on every medication known to treat the disorder, with side effects ranging from exhaustion and depression to lack of concentration. Although his tics subsided, his life was miserable. With a wife and two young children, he had no energy to be the kind of husband and father he wanted to be. He and his wife contacted The HANDLE Institute, and flew to Seattle for an evaluation.

Upon his return home, I called him to find out what he had learned. He told me about the evaluation session, the treatment and follow-up. The treatment was unlike anything we had ever heard about, but it made sense. It didn't involve drugs, only simple exercises and diet supplements. After a few weeks of following the program, he became, as he described it, "a new man." This was all I needed to hear. This is what we wanted for our son.

Our meeting with a HANDLE clinician in a neighboring state lasted several hours. We were told that we could stay in the room with Nicholas, but only to observe. The clinician performed numerous non-invasive neurological tests on him. As observers, the tests seemed unrelated to Nick's condition, and we couldn't help but wonder what benefits could be gained from them. It wasn't until later, during the clinician's discussion of findings with us, that we understood. Then came what can only be described as "unusual," the treatment.

Nick was given a series of exercises that he was to do every day. Not anything strenuous, or physical in any way. They included Face Tapping, where I would gently tap his face in a designated pattern, writing with a pink highlighter with 3-D glasses on, twirling a hula hoop on his arms, and a hand-clapping/whistling game, which I must say we became quite good at! All of these exercises, custom designed to treat his specific issues, took no more than a half an hour a day. The key was to do no more than prescribed, and to be consistent. We didn't miss a day. I will never forget how after only one week of his regimen Nick walked down the hallway with his arms outstretched. "Look at how still I can hold my arms, Mom!" Then I began noticing changes that added up to milestones. He'd come home from school and do his homework by himself. His attention span grew dramatically longer. He'd do chores willingly and stopped interrupting during conversations. That week I threw away his Clonadine. We concluded that medications treat the symptoms; The HANDLE Institute treats the root problem. We continued the exercises for three months, at which time I could honestly say he was "cured."

Since that time, he has maintained honor roll status in school. He is now a well-behaved, intelligent 16 year old that makes his parents so proud.

As parents, we want to think we're doing the perfect job in raising our children. So many times during Nick's childhood I felt like an incompetent mother. Why did he give me such a hard time? Surely, I thought, it must be something I'm doing wrong. He would throw himself down on the ground in a crowded mall, while onlookers gave me disgusted looks and unsolicited advice. His constant interruptions in conversations prompted people to tell me he was impolite. His antics branded him wild and unruly. These are comments that break a mother's heart, for I knew that inside that little body there was another child aching to come out. Now, looking back over the years, I don't feel like a failure. I know that I was a good mother. I took his hand and led him down the path to a happy, healthy and productive future.

A STEP BACKWARD INTO A BETTER TIME

CINDY DALLMANN

"Amazing!" "It's incredible!" "I wouldn't have believed it if I hadn't seen it with my own eyes!" "I am so excited—I can't believe the change in him in such a short amount of time!" "I was so surprised when he came up and initiated a conversation with me. The last time I saw him he wouldn't talk to me or even look at me when I talked to him!" "Seeing him so greatly improved made me want to cry and go up and hug him, but I didn't. I was afraid I would embarrass him. But I'll tell you this, it not only made my day, it made my whole week!"

These are all comments from family and friends about Austin, our 15-year-old son. Superlatives? Yes, but not overstating the case, definitely not. What we've witnessed in Austin's life since we met with Judith Bluestone at The HANDLE Institute in Seattle is nothing short of miraculous. But let me start at the beginning.

Even before he was born, Austin was very active. An older woman once commented that it was probably because he had the umbilical cord wrapped around his neck. I dismissed this as an old wives' tale, but I knew that this was unusually common with the male children in my husband's family. My older son, in fact, had the cord wrapped around his neck when he was born, as had many of his male cousins and uncles. It caused the stillbirth of a second cousin. One doctor suggested that an unusually long umbilical cord, which can easily wrap around the neck of an active baby in utero, might be genetic.

During labor, Austin's heart rate took a dramatic plunge at each contraction. The doctors and nurses were very concerned. They suspected that his oxygen supply was being compromised, and they wanted him delivered as quickly as possible. When his head delivered, they discovered the cord was around his neck not once, but twice! They had to cut the cord before delivering the rest of him. But, according to medical standards, he was considered healthy, so we were not unduly worried about the long-term effects of the restricting cord.

But, babyhood proved traumatic for Austin. Digestive problems caused him to fuss through his first six months. Of course, babies survive colic, so I wasn't too concerned. Just get through these first six months, I thought, and he will grow out of it. But he didn't—his problems multiplied. First, there was teething! Prolonged, agonizing teething, as I had never seen before. Each tooth took at least six months to come in, and after it had been in for several months, it might disappear for a time, and he would have to relive the misery of cutting the same tooth all over again. There were times when he cried almost constantly unless he was nursing, swinging in his baby swing, sucking his pacifier or sleeping. Not that sleeping was much of a break. During the worst of it, he would sleep in 20-minute stretches, then wake up and scream for several hours. I tried liquid pain relievers, but he threw them up. I tried numbing agents, which didn't do a thing to relieve his distress. Several dentists offered to lance his gums, but I knew that would be futile since once a tooth erupted, it was just as likely to disappear again.

Austin was prone to ear infections. It seemed that the more he cried, the more likely he was to end up with one. That, of course, only complicated the situation. I would do all I could to keep him from crying, both for his sake and for the sanity of our family. Austin spent much of his first two years swinging and sucking. How interesting it was to find out later that these two activities were probably critical to his mental development. At that time, I had no idea—I didn't even know he had a neurological problem, let alone how to correct it. In fact, others criticized me for leaving Austin in the swing so much, and I can't count the number of times someone asked when I was going to take the pacifier away. Since it provided my only quiet time, I was not anxious to wean him of either, and I am so very grateful now that I did not. Austin's body was demanding what it needed most, and God was moving us in the right direction despite our lack of knowledge.

Eating was a struggle for Austin from the beginning. As a baby, he threw up much of what he ate, and as he got older, we had to coax food down him. He would say he was hungry, take one bite and then say he was full. Somehow, his stomach just never seemed right.

And we began to notice other things about Austin that were unusual. While he was still crawling, his five-year-old brother accidentally stepped solidly on his right hand with the heel of his cowboy boot on a brick surface. Clearly, this should have hurt, and we hurried to his rescue. But, he didn't cry. In fact, he didn't seem even to be bothered by it. We were amazed. We thought, "Wow, this is one tough kid."

When he started walking, we noticed that his right foot turned in slightly and he seemed a bit awkward. His general coordination seemed lacking somehow. When he would color or draw, he used his left hand, but his right hand would move involuntarily, too. Later, when he was able to express himself well, he once said that his right hand felt as if were asleep all the time. I questioned him further, and realized that he could feel pressure on his right side, but the sensations were different from those he felt on his left. He could use his right hand, but it was not well coordinated.

When Austin was four, he began to have "spells"—he seemed to simply blank out. He was still standing, looking at me, but he wouldn't respond. And then, when it was over, he couldn't remember anything that I had said. These "spells" would last between 15 seconds and one minute. During these occurrences, Austin would sometimes walk backward a few steps. One day, while standing on a chair helping me make cookies, he backed off the chair, giving me quite a scare.

We took Austin to our doctor, who referred us to a neurologist. The neurologist conducted an EEG, which revealed some right lobe/left lobe crossover irregularities. The neurologist didn't think things looked too serious, labeled his "spells" psychomotor seizures, and said that a CAT scan or MRI would be necessary if the seizures continued. The only solution offered by the neurologist was drug therapy—Ritalin.

We wanted to avoid drugs. We felt they would only mask the problem, and we were concerned about side effects. We took Austin, instead, to our chiropractor. He found that Austin's top two vertebrae were out, and he could see why Austin was having problems. Once adjusted, the seizures went away completely, but just for a time. Though he had other seizures, ranging from lesser occipital lobe seizures to severe, generalized, grand mal seizures, it seemed, for a time, as if frequent chiropractic care could keep them under control.

Austin's obsessive-compulsive symptoms began around the age of 12. In retrospect, some symptoms had been there since he was little, but we didn't recognize them for what they were, until they became severe. Austin could become obsessed with an irrational thought. It would control his thinking, as if his mind was stuck in a gear and he couldn't shift, or stuck in the mud, spinning tires, digging the rut deeper and deeper. The intrusive thought made it difficult for him to concentrate on anything else. Logic provided no relief; we couldn't talk him out of the obsession.

Austin felt as if he needed to be accountable to his father, his brother or myself at all times, to be sure he hadn't done anything wrong. Someone had to be with him day and night. He slept poorly, sometimes not going to sleep until 4 a.m., and often waking up more than a dozen times to make sure I was watching him. We took him to a highly recommended, very sensitive counselor, but for some reason the sessions were traumatic for Austin. In the end, the counselor told us that we would probably need to look into drug therapy before continuing with him because of the way Austin was responding. Again, we were extremely hesitant to start drug therapy. We had read about the possible side effects of the drugs used to treat Obsessive-Compulsive Disorder (OCD). The risks seemed too great.

By the time Austin was 14, our chiropractor could no longer keep the seizure activity under control. He suggested an MRI to check for lesions or other possible causes of the seizures. The MRI did show evidence of a problem, so we made an appointment with a neurologist, who showed the MRI to us. We were shocked. The left hemisphere of Austin's brain was considerably smaller than the right. Some of the tissue was missing. Well, that explained why we had noticed that his head seemed small for his age, and when we rubbed over his skull, there seemed to be extra loose skin, particularly on the left side. Since the left side of the brain controls the right side of the body, it also explained Austin's awkwardness and lack of feeling on his right side. Apparently, Austin had suffered a stroke at birth, from the cord around his neck, and the brain tissue that should have been fed oxygen from the middle cerebral artery, was degenerated. We have since learned that oxygen deprivation is not uncommon during the birthing process, with varying degrees of neurological damage resulting.

The neurologist said that there was nothing to be done about the smaller left hemisphere of the brain or the effects of the stroke. Growing new tissue was not possible, so we would simply need to learn to live with the effects. He surmised that the stroke was probably the cause of the seizures, and most likely the cause of the OCD, too. He did another EEG and recommended drug therapy for the seizures. Again, we passed on the medication.

But we did believe that answers were out there. Then, after many dozens of hours on the Internet, we hit upon the website for The HANDLE Institute. I had been researching seizures when I brought up an article Judith Bluestone had written. It was different from anything else I had read; it was so logical and encouraging. I was thrilled! Here was the first real hope I'd had in a long time. I cried as I read the testimonials on the website. I called the office and talked to someone there, and through the HANDLE referral list, I contacted other mothers of children with OCD who had used HANDLE's method of treatment with great success.

After much prayer, we made an appointment to see Judith in October. But, she was in Seattle and we were in Douglas, Nebraska. We knew that to be able to go, God would have to provide the finances for the whole trip. That would be our confirmation that it was the right thing. By October, He had provided free plane tickets, free hotel lodging and $3,500 cash to cover expenses. That was proof enough for us!

October came none too soon. Austin was having a grand mal seizure about every two weeks, his OCD was controlling our lives completely, and he had developed photophobia and phonophobia (light and sound sensitivity) to such an extent that he was unable to read, watch TV, use the computer—or much of anything for that matter. The days were long for Austin, and though we tried, our attempts at relief were futile. Essentially, Austin followed me around the house, and sat and watched to make sure I was watching him. Austin is a bright child. It was so hard to see him that way.

We were concerned about how Austin might react to Judith based on his response to the counselor who worked with him on his OCD. But, we didn't need to worry. Both she and Kavita Dinghra, an advanced HANDLE intern who worked with Austin, had a non-intimidating and reassuring way with Austin—and with us. The assessment and evaluation were amazing!

Using simple, non-threatening techniques and adjusting the environment to meet Austin's needs, they were able to encourage Austin to remove, momentarily, his ear plugs and his heavily tinted sunglasses that were his shields against the bombardment of sound and light on his hypersensitive senses. They then pinpointed the exact areas where Austin struggled. Judith's knowledge of neurological disorders was astounding. Finally, we had answers to questions we had been asking for many years, some since his birth. She provided explanations in clear, logical terms, and it all made perfect sense.

Yet, I had to admit to Judith that the therapies seemed so extremely simple that I had trouble believing, considering the serious nature of Austin's problems, that they could really make a difference. She smiled and remarked that people sometimes forego the benefits of HANDLE's Gentle Enhancement therapies because they are so locked into a "no-pain-no-gain" philosophy.

But, it didn't take long to make a believer out of me; changes became apparent almost immediately. On our flight home, one week later, Austin played his GameBoy for an hour on the plane, something he had not been able to do in over a year. In fact, I don't know why I bothered to pack it, but I was sure glad I did. What a thrill to see progress so quickly! We couldn't wait to see what six months, even six weeks, would bring.

Within one week, Austin's sleep had improved dramatically, and he began sleeping, a sound sleep, 10 to 11 hours a night. He wasn't waking me up more than once or twice a night, if that. He would even stay in bed after he knew I was up—that hadn't happened in years!

Soon, I had the sense that Austin had taken a giant

step backward into a better time. He began, once again, to fill his days with writing, GameBoy, guitar playing, reading—just books with large print, but we were thrilled nonetheless—drawing, and, of course, his HANDLE exercises. Gradually, he increased the number of repetitions of each exercise he was able to do. We found a way to make the Peacemaker Massage comfortable for him, and he began to enjoy it. In fact, when we we're done, he often offered to do it for me! And then he asked, begged really, for me to do his reflexology longer. We'd save it for last—Austin calls it "dessert." I am amazed, still, at how easy it all is and how little time it takes.

Until this time, every waking hour, even inside with the blinds closed, Austin had been wearing dark glasses to protect his eyes from the light; two pair if he ventured out. About a week after returning home, I noticed that he would push them up for a few minutes off and on throughout the day. Then he began to say that they were too dark. We got him some lightly tinted ones, but within a couple of weeks, he shed those too. Now Austin plays basketball, mid-day sun shining, with no sunglasses at all! Amazing!

It took about six weeks for the earplugs, which he wore constantly, to come out for good. Only a hint of sound sensitivity remains. Austin is so relieved to be living life without the extra pressure of the sunglasses and earplugs, and more importantly, without the awkward feeling that he is being stared at wherever he goes.

Then, unexpectedly, Austin decided that he wanted to knit—of all things! Secretly, I was concerned that he would be discouraged, that it would be too frustrating given the sensitivity of his eyes and poor right-side fine motor skills. My knowledge of knitting is limited, and I couldn't figure out how to teach him to do it left-handed. I was ready to give up, but my tenacious son decided he'd just learn to do it right handed. It was a struggle, and I know with certainty I would have given up had I been in his place. In fact, I had to work hard to suppress my will to suggest that he just quit and try again in six months. But, two days later, he was doing so well that he started on his first project—a red, white and blue throw. We were amazed, greatly encouraged, and maybe just a bit concerned by his dogged determination.

Austin's cousin, who is his age and loves to read, had her nose stuck in a book a good deal of the time she was last here for a visit. When Austin finally got tired of watching her enjoy herself, by herself, he dug out a book of about 100 pages and read it in two days. He was so encouraged that he read another over the next day and a half. Within two weeks he had read eight books—more than he's read in the last four years all together, I'm sure.

Austin began to separate himself from us and become his own person; his anxiety began to ease. While at a friend's house, watching the ball game on TV, our friend offered to hire Austin to rake leaves. "Ya, right," we all thought. Well, Aus went out and raked by himself for about half an hour. We watched from the window, and not once did he check to see that we were watching. It was an unbelievably huge step forward.

Shopping had always been traumatic, but this year, at the holidays, we shopped—eight hours and 17 stores! It was like old times, only better. We had a ball!

Now, he walks the church halls by himself, even initiating conversations with adults; unthinkable just six months ago. Out to dinner with family friends, Austin sat, three chairs away from his Dad, with a friend he hadn't seen in two years. He ordered the meal by himself, even asking questions of a very grumpy waitress. This may not seem a big deal for most 15 year olds, but to our family and the friends who observed, it was huge. I thought it would be many months before he'd risk something like that with a stranger. I feel as if the umbilical cord has finally been cut. He has gone from not wanting to be out of my sight to going outside to play ball several times a day, sometimes for over an hour at a time.

And how thankful we are that God allowed us to find HANDLE when we did—for Austin's sake. With the turn of the new year, life brought us one traumatic experience after another, including illnesses and the loss of Austin's grandmother. In addition to the stress, Austin was unable to do his exercises consistently, and we thought he would regress. I don't want to think how he might have handled all this if he hadn't first been to HANDLE, but, to our amazement and delight, Austin continued to take steps that were almost shocking to me. Through it all, he was so casual, as if his continued growth was the most natural thing in the world.

Late one afternoon, he asked if he could go hunting. He has never gone hunting by himself because he didn't want to be alone. I said he could, but, oh, me of little faith, didn't expect him to get far. He walked a half mile out and arrived back home after it was so dark I was ready to go out looking for him. He acted as if I was being silly to worry and make a fuss about him going so far. So I took my cue from him and allowed him to go again the next afternoon. Twenty minutes after he left, he came back, proudly carrying a rabbit. (Sorry, bunny lovers, but we have so terribly many around here that they kill a lot of our plants and trees, which are sparse and hard to grow. The rabbits multiply, well, like rabbits, and are hard to control.) Austin hunted three days in a row.

In the past, as Austin prepared for hunting, he expected me to help with his layers of clothes: boots, coat, vest, etc., and then he'd worry that his boots were too tight and have me redo them at least once. On these latest occasions, however, he took care of pretty much everything himself. He says he's just growing up. We think it's more than that.

Now, if you ask Aus, his crowning achievement took place when he got his learner's permit to drive. To be eligible, Austin had to be seizure-free for three months. Three months and one day after his last seizure, Austin did it! On his own, he filled out the paper work, communicated with the licensing personnel and missed only one out of 25 questions! Several months ago, when he went into the licensing department to pick up the booklet to begin studying for the test, he was so nervous he could hardly breathe, and that was with his dad right beside him. This time he was willing, in fact anxious—with just a healthy bit of nerves.

Since we began our HANDLE program six months ago, Austin has had only three seizures, and they've all been relatively mild. And with each, we feel we've been able to track back to the origin. The seizure that he had the day after he earned his learner's permit was most likely due to oncoming headlights while driving in the dark, coupled with the excitement of the test itself. But in this, Austin wasn't even sure that he'd had a seizure until he got up four hours later. The day following a seizure, Austin is generally hypersensitive, but this day he was able to function normally, and we even kept our plans to eat out in a restaurant.

Over the years, Austin's chiropractor encouraged him to work harder at standing up straight to keep his neck in alignment. Austin tried, but it just didn't happen. But now, with the help of improved muscle tone—and confidence—Austin stands taller. He is more independent, socially adept and verbally competent. Austin's favorite cousin told her mom that she can't believe Austin is the same person—so calm and laid back.

On every front, we are encouraged. We continue to thank God for you, Judith—your wonderful, brilliant mind and loving heart. As I have said many times before, and I'm sure I will say many times again, we will be forever grateful. You have an amazing ability to make the fuzzy become clear, and we are so glad to have had the privilege of working with you.

Our HANDLE experience has been life changing, not just for Austin, but for all of us. I feel better than I have in years. Based on the wonder we have witnessed over the last six months, we are confident that Austin's neurological development will continue. Our future is bright and exciting. Austin has been given a second chance at life—something we wish, passionately, for everyone with neuro-developmental problems. We recommend HANDLE, with complete confidence, to anyone who will listen; there *is* hope in situations called "hopeless."

THE HUMAN SYSTEM—THE SOCIAL SYSTEM
A POSTSCRIPT BY JUDITH BLUESTONE

Nick and his hyperactive behaviors signaled a system that was out of order, one that was responding willy-nilly to bits of information without waiting to receive those bits that would fill in the gaps and allow for integrated processing. His tics reflected weaknesses in particular parts of his systems, which, coupled with an inability to determine which part of him needed to respond to bothersome input, resulted in movements that were out of his control.

Medication might have increased the speed of his processing so that he received more information before responding, and his response might have been organized. But there were still those few channels of information that were weak and received external stimulation as annoyances. These channels could not share their information readily, and could not keep their irritation from spreading, via other nerves, to different systems, resulting in vocal tics and motor tics. Nick was no longer in control of his own body.

And Austin may never have been in control of his own body, as each movement he made, even in utero, conflicted with his basic need for survival. He was literally in a double bind, with his umbilical cord tied twice around his neck, and his basic instincts and reflexes telling him to move. Austin's survival instinct continued to restrict his behaviors. As demands upon his systems increased, his autonomic nervous system won over all others, putting him in a nearly continual state of fight-or-flight, and shutting down to the extent that seizures became a frightening backdrop to life. How could he not have obsessive-compulsive thoughts and behaviors, with such a battle raging within. His two dissonant cerebral hemispheres fought one another, leaving him unable to make a decision other than to safely repeat what he had just done or thought. He needed more than just the impetus to move on; he needed, first, the strength to support this brave venture. A strength he could get only by gently enhancing each of his weak systems and guiding them to integrate their information.

In the stories of these two boys, nearly men, is more than a message of hope for individuals diagnosed with Tourette's Syndrome, or thought to have an attentional disorder, or presenting with obsessive-compulsive behaviors. There is also a parable. As a society, we have been demanding answers before we have the necessary and sufficient information to process them into meaningful results. We hastily push the process through the system without regard to blockages and leakages of information. We respond in the same way, over and over again, because we are stuck in a pattern, no matter how dysfunctional. We are reluctant to expend resources on the preventative and rehabilitative measures needed to resolve issues at their roots. In our unwillingness, society pays a dear price as we live with the truth of exploding drug and gang cultures, rising population of teen mothers and burgeoning prison populations.

Is there a way out?

From our original parable, *The Story of the Churkendoose*, the fox *is* in the henhouse, chasing this way and that, trying to catch whomever he can. Squawking and shrieking and running will not chase the fox away. This fox is within everyone who will not accept that faster is slower; that quick fixes and medications to mask symptoms and programs to control behaviors are not working. We must stop our societal obsessive-compulsive disorder of continuing to do what we have found is dysfunctional. We must stop responding to syndromes with only partial information, but work collaboratively for integrated, holistic care to resolve our problems. We must discern which differences are bothersome and which are merely quirks. Our goal must be to help each individual to be as functional as he or she can, not to be as similar to his peers or family members as possible. We must open windows, not close doors. As a society, we must acknowledge that we have had a bad case of the tics, and we are now ready to learn from the stories of the Churkendeese and from all of those who have been able to help individuals move from dysfunction to function, naturally.

EPILOGUE:
WITHOUT "ALWAYS,"
"NEVER" AND "IMPOSSIBLE"

"**W**ho are the people HANDLE cannot help?" I receive this question frequently. At first, I had difficulty answering this question, since I, too, am in awe of the scope of issues that HANDLE practitioners are helping to resolve. Yet, upon reviewing the circumstances of those who do not make significant gains, I've realized that there are some, and they fall into four categories:

1) People who will not do their programs.

2) People who do not accept the paradigm shift to Gentle Enhancement, and thus overwork and stress the systems they are trying to strengthen.

3) People whose identities are entangled in their roles as a "disabled" person or as the caregiver of someone with a disability. Their fear of positive change, thus loss of identity, keeps them from successfully implementing their program.

4) People who are unaware, however blissfully or tragically, that alternatives to conventional treatments are available.

For some in the first group, HANDLE *does* subscribe to the "no pain, no gain" philosophy—but, only in the sense that these people may need to feel the pain of their problems more acutely before they are motivated to change. Until an individual feels the need to change, he or she may be unready for help.

Others who do not implement their programs may feel that the approach is just too simple. One youngster with whom I worked would not cooperate with his parents on his home-based program. His non-compliance, however, was not for lack of pain—he felt, quite profoundly, the pain of his dyslexia in contrast to his intellectual giftedness. However, he thought that HANDLE therapy was "bogus," and no matter how we explained the causal connections between his weak and irregular systems and his reading challenges, he would not accept that a few simple activities could be a catalyst to reading. He wanted to get on with learning to read, even though the tutors and reading programs had not helped.

Finally, he agreed to cooperate, but only to prove that the program was "bogus." We told him to stick with it for six weeks, and he would see a significant difference. At the end of the six weeks, he was reading! He proved to himself, and to others, that the programs will work—if they are implemented.

The second group—those who can't accept Gentle Enhancement—presents a greater challenge. These people may need to wait for the proof—the publication of research on how HANDLE alters the structure and function of the brain and central nervous system. Perhaps as they read the scientific perspective on the importance of Gentle Enhancement and of efficiency, rather than effectiveness, in getting a job done—perhaps then they will accept the truth in the statement that nervous systems under stress do not get stronger.

And when the concept of Gentle Enhancement gets lost, as often happens in group settings, other problems arise. When performing the exercises with peers or colleagues, a sense of competitiveness may motivate one person to stress his systems to prove he is as capable as another. Or, another may not reap the full benefit from an activity because she feels justified in stopping when a classmate stops. To achieve results in group situations, each member of the group must acknowledge the differences among individuals, with respect and acceptance of diversity.

The third group has a special place in my heart. These individuals have grieved the dreams that were "stolen" from them. They have invested resources in providing the best care for their loved ones. They have abandoned their own social lives to be caregivers. They have done this for years, and they recognize that they will continue to make sacrifices and remain vigilant over the safety of their loved ones for the rest of their lives.

Then their disabled family member begins to show signs of growth, of improvement! What does that mean for physical safety? Will the "poor dear" be ready for the pain of rejection as he bumps up against society, unaccustomed to such interaction? And, what now is the role of the caregiver? What friends and what job opportunities have been lost during the years of care giving? The individuals in this group need help from counselors and friends who can support them through their sojourn in this new and frightening territory.

The fourth group—those unacquainted with the range of choices in treatments—may be locked into the status quo of labels that describe inadequacy, predict failure and limit aspirations, or they may be vulnerable to the prejudices that are cultivated by societal influence. This group needs the courage to explore a new model, a fresh worldview. In this, they can appreciate that it is the fear of difference, rather than respect for individuality, that hinders growth. And not just for the rejected individual, but also for the society whose fear causes the rejection. The stories of triumph compiled in this anthology help to dispel prejudice by granting respect for individuals whose situations might otherwise be feared.

Perhaps this work, *The Churkendoose Anthology*, will introduce hope to individuals and society as a whole, and provide the impetus for this paradigm shift. And as a result of this work, perhaps everyone *can* benefit from HANDLE, once they have accepted its basic premises and are inspired to improve their futures. To this aim, *The Churkendoose Anthology* mounts anecdotal evidence in support of a **H**olistic **A**pproach to **N**euro**D**evelopment and **L**earning **E**fficiency—HANDLE. The HANDLE paradigm applies neuroscience to bring about integrated mind-bodies, enabled to accept life's challenges. And it promises empowered families and communities to find within themselves the tools to move from dysfunction to function, from despair to fulfillment. The people whose stories are presented here lead the way.

This anthology toasts to the future around the corner. As my father instilled in me in my childhood, without the words "always," "never" and "impossible," the possibilities are unlimited.

APPENDIX A:

SELECTED EXERCISES

CRAZY STRAW

BENEFITS:

When you examine the importance of sucking in human development, it is truly profound. Not only do we suck for nourishment, we accomplish many other amazing things:

♦ When we integrate the two sides of our mouth and cheeks in sucking, we stimulate the two cerebral hemispheres in a coordinated rhythmic fashion, enhancing their integration. We rely on this interhemispheric integration to process language, balance our instincts with logic, and so many other functions frequently compromised in neurobehavioral disorders and brain injury.

♦ As we suck, many of our cranial nerves are stimulated, and they in turn help regulate many aspects of our vision, including the ability of our eyes to converge, that is, focus together on a target.

♦ Stimulation of the trigeminal and facial nerves directly stimulates structures in the middle ear, dampening the volume of the sounds we hear. It is common knowledge that chewing gum or sucking helps people tolerate the pressure change in their ears during take-off and landing on flights. And through a connection in the part of the midbrain called the colliculus, visual focus directs auditory focus, connecting the work of the crazy straw in improving visual focus with reduction of distractibility to noise in the environment.

♦ The crazy straw activity improves tongue and lip control and coordinated breathing, all of which support articulation.

♦ It is a little known fact that strengthening any set of sphincter muscles, such as the lips while sucking, strengthens all of the sphincters in our body, such as the iris which controls the pupils of the eyes and, of course, the bowel and bladder.

♦ One reason that people can become sensitive to light is if their two eyes do not team in the processing of visual images which, of course, is based on perception of light and darkness. In addition, the pupils may have a reduced degree of reactivity to light. Drinking through the straw enhances both visual teaming and the pupil's reactivity to light, and thereby reduces light sensitivity.

♦ Sucking, especially early in life, stimulates the pituitary gland for balanced hormone production, including the human growth factor hormone.

MATERIALS:

You will need a crazy straw (a plastic straw with curls or twists and a small diameter), and a clear drink. Water is recommended, since it is essential to healthy brain and body functions. Also, it is easier to clean a crazy straw if it is used only for water.

Because the twists and turns of the crazy straw create resistance in sucking, people whose ears are very sensitive, should use a regular straw, particularly if using the crazy straw causes ear pain.

PROCEDURE:

Hold the straw in the center of your mouth, and sip and swallow, allowing a rhythmic pattern to develop if you can. You will benefit more from doing this with your eyes closed unless your eyes tend to over-converge. If you have a tendency for, or a history of, crossed eyes, do not close them as you suck. Instead, look at a distant object while drinking.

VARIATIONS:

♦ Even if there is a fear of aspirating liquids, receiving the benefits from sucking is still possible. Using a straw to create suction, transfer small bits of paper from the table to make a mosaic on a larger piece of paper. Or use the straw to pick up a light object, such as a paper napkin, and transfer it from one side of your tray to the other.

♦ If you cannot swallow thin liquids, use a thick beverage and drink it through a regular straw.

PRECAUTIONS:

Be sure to rinse out the straw well after each drink, so harmful bacteria do not build up in the loops.

If you are pregnant, do not engage in this intense sucking, as it may stimulate contractions.

Face tapping

Benefits:

This activity awakens, organizes, integrates and relaxes the trigeminal nerve, one of the twelve cranial nerves. This may produce many benefits, among them, alleviation of headaches, integration of facial and general tactile sensations, reduction of the pain of TMJ, support for speech production, relief of facial tics and paralysis, and an increase in facial muscle tone for expression of affect. Face Tapping frequently gives rise to a sense of calmness.

Materials:

You will need just your hands or the hands of a helper.

Procedure:

Find a comfortable position for this activity. You may tap your own face, or have someone do it for you. If you tap your own face, it may help to do it in front of a mirror.

Using two fingers on each hand, tap rapidly and rhythmically, alternating from one hand to the other, taking "baby steps" along the trigeminal nerve as shown in the illustration on the following page. The tempo of this tapping should approximate the beat in *Twinkle Twinkle Little Star*. The energy involved in each tap should be enough to produce a sound if you were to tap on a tabletop. Your goal is to stimulate the nerves between the skin and the bone. You will know that the tapping pressure is right if you feel a tingling or a sense of vitality to the face after tapping, but no discomfort or pain. Adjust the tap, or guide your helper to tap to your comfort level.

The tapping pattern should consistently follow the same pattern, so the brain begins to anticipate the stimulation. Here is the recommended sequence:

1) From the temple along the eyebrows, to the midpoint between the eyebrows, up to the hairline and return by the same path to the temple.

2) From the temple down across the top of the cheek-bone to the bridge of the nose and back to the temple.

3) From the temple down along the bottom edge of the cheekbone, along the "moustache area," and in to meet below the nose. Then return to the temple, tapping.

4) From the temple downward to the rearmost corner of the lower jaw then forward on the gum line of the lower jaw to meet tapping hands in the space between the lower lip and the chin. Return, tapping, to the temple.

5) From the temple around behind the ears, where the eye-glass arms would rest on the bone, very close to but not touching the ear. Return, tapping, to the temple. This last pathway is not on the trigeminal nerve proper, but enhances hearing via bone conduction.

VARIATIONS ON FACE TAPPING:

♦ If you find the face tapping uncomfortable, even after reducing the intensity of the tap, tap through a cool cloth placed over the face.

♦ If you have long fingernails, use the knuckles of your first two fingers to tap.

♦ If you have a severe sinus condition, reduce the intensity of the tapping, but do try to tap, as it may help to promote sinus drainage.

♦ If you are sensitive to smell, make sure your helper is not wearing highly scented hand lotion or sleeves that are scented by fabric softener, smoke, or any other scent you find offensive.

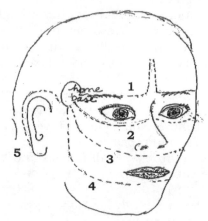

HUG AND TUG

BENEFITS:

This activity enhances interhemispheric integration and articulation. It is also useful in promoting differentiation of fingers, one from the other, and from one hand to the other. Hug and Tug strengthens muscle tone of the fingers, stimulates reflex points for the sinuses, jaw and mouth, integrates tactile sensations in the hands, enhances proprioceptive input in the fingers and hands, and may also calm and focus the individual.

MATERIALS:

You will need only your own hands and possibly the hands of a helper. If your helper's fingers are much larger than yours, you may also need sturdy soft yarn or a pipecleaner.

PROCEDURE:

With your arms resting on a supportive surface or placed lightly against your lower ribcage, interlock your index fingers, holding your hands so they meet at the midline of your body.

Squeeze and pull with your interlocked index fingers— one relaxes as the other pulls, then the other relaxes and the other finger pulls. Both of your hands and arms remain virtually motionless and relaxed—only the fingers are moving a bit.

Repeat the back and forth pull-release three or four times as the index fingers stay hooked together.

Unhook your index fingers and interlock your middle fingers, and repeat.

Continue with all fingers and then, finally, hug and tug your thumbs.

VARIATIONS:

♦ Allow your helper to engage and manipulate your fingers, each hand separately first and then both hands together, with your hands crossed over the midline of your body. To accomplish this, with your finger interlocked with your helper's, the helper gently presses on the nail of your finger as it is wedged between her index and middle fingers. At the same time she presses with her thumb on your index finger segment closest to your hand, while giving the hug and tug squeeze.

♦ If your fingers are too small to interlock comfortably with your helper's, your helper can use a loop of yarn or a pipe-cleaner around the middle segment of your finger. She will then need to hug and tug on the yarn with her other hand while wedging the finger segments, as above.

♦ Pair squeezes of interlocked fingers with phrases or words.

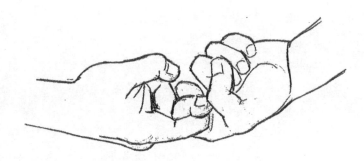

APPENDIX B:

CLINICAL PROCEDURES

CLINICAL PROCEDURES

EVALUATION

The HANDLE evaluation begins with an intake questionnaire and a verbal exploration of history and presenting concerns. The HANDLE practitioner guides the two-hour assessment, in the presence of the client's parents, caregivers or support persons, in a manner that is non-judgmental, non-stressful and affirming.

Throughout the evaluation, the HANDLE practitioner engages the client in a series of varied activities while noting response patterns and analyzing strengths and weaknesses in the client's processing. The practitioner employs observational assessment, rather than standardized testing, to ascertain which functional areas are inefficient, which are obstructed.

Following the evaluation phase, the client enjoys some free time, while the practitioner develops a comprehensive profile of the client's core neurological processing. This neurodevelopmental profile traces presenting concerns back to their origins, through the paths of vision and audition, proprioception, kinesthesia and vestibular functioning, to the most foundational level of touch, taste and smell. It incorporates the processes of attention, differentiation, lateralization and integration as well. The root causes of perplexing behavior and poor learning patterns are brought to light, and a picture of the dynamic interaction of neurological functioning emerges.

The practitioner then uses knowledge of the client's developmental history, including to gestational influences, nutrition, allergies, other special health problems, and more to ascertain the total environment in which these roots developed. These factors, too, become part of the profile, not to place blame, but to discern if other procedures or complementary health measures should be explored. This comprehensive profile then provides a roadmap to guide the creation of a therapeutic treatment plan unique to each client.

PRESENTATION OF RESULTS

The client and family receive a thorough discussion of the results, an explanation of the recommendations and skilled guidance in the implementation of their program. The practitioner may also make nutritional recommendations or suggest temporary environmental accommodations, such as reducing extraneous sounds in the surrounding or altering lighting, as necessary. HANDLE provides clients virtually all the special tools required for implementation of the activities.

THE HOME TREATMENT PROGRAM

Each program is customized for effective application in the client's home or other supportive setting. Videotapes made of the clinical sessions provide the client a tool for easy reference at home. Programs generally require less than half an hour daily. The recommended activities are simple to perform, and can be done as a sequence or broken into several clusters, depending upon individual preferences and schedules. Some activities may require support from a caregiver. The focus is always on Gentle Enhancement to strengthen the client's neurological functioning without producing stress. To this effect, some programs incorporate Mental Rehearsal to allow a client to progress by watching others perform specific activities.

FINE-TUNING AND PROGRAM REVIEWS

Within two weeks of starting a HANDLE home-treatment program, a fine-tuning session ensures understanding and correct application of the activities. It also provides an opportunity to adjust the program to the client's progress. Additional program review sessions are recommended every four to six weeks. Many clients see significant results within the first few months, but we encourage each client to benefit from six-months of fine-tuning. If an in-person visit isn't possible, your practitioner will work with you to find an alternative such videotape and an e-mail or phone discussion.

ADDITIONAL SUPPORT

Most clients achieve their goals through the home-implemented programs. Occasionally, clients may benefit from therapy sessions with their practitioners, or other on-site work to determine issues of mismatch between the client's system and the general environment. HANDLE practitioners are dedicated to meeting whatever level of support our clients need.

IS HANDLE RIGHT FOR YOU?

To help you decide if the HANDLE approach can address your concerns, we offer additional information at community presentations, on audiotape, by e-mail and telephone and on our website. In addition, we can provide you with contact information for Certified HANDLE Practitioners, as well as phone numbers of clients who have been through their HANDLE program and are willing to share their thoughts on the process and the results. To find out more, contact us at:

The HANDLE Institute International, LLC
1300 Dexter Ave. North
Suite 110
Seattle, WA 98109

Phone: (206) 204-6000
Fax: (206) 860-3505
Email: support@handle.org
Web: www.handle.org

The Churkendoose Anthology

ORDER FORM

Order on-line (www.handle.org) or use the form below

Mail : The HANDLE Institute International, LLC
1300 Dexter Avenue North, Suite 110
Seattle, WA 98109
Phone: (206) 204-6000 (9am -5pm PST Mon.through Fri.)
Fax: (206) 860-3505

Price $15.95 (U.S.) in Print $21.95 on Audio CD

Quantity _____ In Print _____ Audio CD

Total price _____

Shipping and handling _____
(Within USA & Canada: $4 1st copy plus $1.50 each additional copy
Outside USA & Canada: $12 1st copy plus $4 each additional copy)

Subtotal _____

WA State residents add 8.9 % sales tax _____

Total _____

Address:

Name _____

Address _____

City, State Zip _____

Phone_____ E-mail_____

Ship to:

Name _____

Address _____

City, State Zip _____

Payment method:

☐ Check enclosed

☐ Master Card   ☐ VISA   ☐ Discover   ☐ American Express

Card # _____

Expiration _____

Name on Card _____

Introducing The Churkendoose Project!

The Churkendoose Project is a nonprofit 501(c)(3) organization founded to provide information about the challenges people with neurodevelopmental differences face and therapies that gently enhance neurodevelopment and learning efficiency; to promote research and professional interest in these therapies; and to provide financial assistance to people who cannot afford therapy.

Your tax-deductible gift will provide **GRANTS** to non-profit organizations that serve people with neurodevelopmental challenges.

These grants will provide funds for

• **FINANCIAL AID** to individuals who cannot afford a HANDLE program or other holistic, complementary therapy

• **SCHOLARSHIPS** to individuals who cannot afford HANDLE professional training or training in other complementary therapies

• **FINANCIAL ASSISTANCE** to HANDLE advocates to speak at conferences and other educational events.

The Churkendoose Project will only fund non-drug, non-invasive, non-aversive therapies and treatments.

Apply for assistance, volunteer, or donate by writing to
The Churkendoose Project
10169 New Hampshire Avenue #145
Silver Spring, MD 20903
www.churkendoose.org